Northern Ireland since 1968

Making Contemporary Britain

General Editor: Anthony Seldon
Consultant Editor: Peter Hennessy

Published

Northern Ireland since 1968
Paul Arthur and Keith Jeffery

Britain and the Falklands War
Lawrence Freedman

Forthcoming

British General Elections since 1945
David Butler

Suez 1956
David Carlton

British Defence Policy since 1945
Michael Dockrill

Crime and Policing since 1945
Terence Morris

Institute of Contemporary British History
34 Tavistock Square, London WC1H 9EZ

Northern Ireland since 1968

Paul Arthur and Keith Jeffery

Basil Blackwell

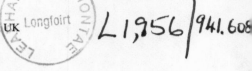

British Library Cataloguing in Publication Data
Arthur, Paul, *1945–*
    Northern Ireland since 1968. – (Making
    contemporary Britain).
    1. Northern Ireland – Politics and
    government – 1969–
    I. Title   II. Jeffery, Keith   III. Series
    941.60824   DA990.U46
    ISBN 0-631-16141-4
    ISBN 0-631-16061-2 Pbk

Library of Congress Cataloging in Publication Data
Arthur, Paul, 1945–
    Northern Ireland since 1968.
    (Making contemporary Britain)
    Bibliography: p.
    Includes index.
    1. Northern Ireland – History – 1969–
I. Jeffery, Keith.   II. Title.   III. Series.
DA990.U46A75   1988   941.6082´4   87-35456
ISBN 0-631-16141-4
ISBN 0-631-16061-2 (pbk.)

Typeset in 11 on 13pt Ehrhardt
by Joshua Associates Ltd, Oxford
Printed in Great Britain by Page Bros (Norwich) Ltd

Contents

General Editor's Preface vi

List of Abbreviations viii

1 Introduction 1

2 The Northern Ireland Political Landscape 5

3 A Place Apart 21

4 Catholic Politics 33

5 Protestant Politics 46

6 Keeping the Peace 62

7 The International Dimension 77

8 Conclusion 93

Appendix I Deaths Caused by the Violence in
Northern Ireland 98

Appendix II The Anglo-Irish Agreement 99

Outline Chronology 109

Dramatis Personae 113

Further Reading 116

Index 117

General Editor's Preface

The Institute of Contemporary British History's series *Making Contemporary Britain* is aimed at undergraduates, sixth-formers and others interested in learning more about topics in postwar British history. In the series, authors are less attempting to break new ground than to present clear and balanced overviews of the state of knowledge on each of the topics.

The ICBH was founded in October 1986 with the objective of promoting the study at every level of British history since 1945. To that end it publishes books and a quarterly journal, *Contemporary Record*, it organizes seminars and conferences for sixth-formers, undergraduates, researchers and teachers of postwar history; and it runs a number of research programmes and other activities.

A central belief in the ICBH's work is that postwar history is too often neglected in schools, institutes of higher education and beyond. The ICBH acknowledges the validity of the arguments against the study of recent history, notably the problems of bias, of overly subjective teaching and writing, and the difficulties of perspective. But it believes that the values of studying postwar history outweigh the drawbacks, and that the health and future of a liberal democracy require that its citizens know more about the most recent past of their country than the limited knowledge possessed by British citizens, young and old, today. Indeed, the ICBH believes that the dangers of political indoctrination are higher where the young are *not* informed of the recent past.

In this book two Northern Ireland specialists, Paul Arthur and Keith Jeffery, examine the recent history of that most intractable of all British problems, the Northern Ireland question.

Rather than provide another chronological account, their approach is in the main thematic. Chapter 1, however, provides a brief historical outline of the principal events from the re-emergence of violence in the late 1960s to the period following the Anglo-Irish Accord. The themes the authors address are the social and economic aspects of the problem, international and military dimensions, religious and nationalist perspectives. The authors conclude with an analysis of some possible 'solutions' to the problem, and offer balanced appraisals of the likelihood of the success of these courses of action.

Anthony Seldon

List of Abbreviations

CDU	Campaign for Democracy in Ulster
DUP	Democratic Unionist Party
IIP	Irish Independence Party
INLA	Irish National Liberation Army
IRA	Irish Republican Army
IRSP	Irish Republican Socialist Party
NICRA	Northern Ireland Civil Rights Association
NILP	Northern Ireland Labour Party
NUPRG	New Ulster Political Research Group
PD	People's Democracy
PIRA	Provisional Irish Republican Army
PSF	Provisional Sinn Fein
PUP	Protestant Unionist Party
RUC	Royal Ulster Constabulary
SDLP	Social Democratic and Labour Party
UDA	Ulster Defence Association
UDR	Ulster Defence Regiment
UPRG	Ulster Political Research Group
USCA	Ulster Special Constabulary Association
UUP	Ulster Unionist Party
UUUC	United Ulster Unionist Council
UVF	Ulster Volunteer Force
UWC	Ulster Workers' Council
VPP	Volunteer Political Party
VUP	Vanguard Unionist Party

1 Introduction

One of the clichés concerning the Northern Ireland problem contends that if all the publications, the explanations, the analyses and the solutions to the problem were put side by side they would span the circumference of the world. The problem still remains obscure to many and we believe there is room for yet another examination of 'the Troubles'.

In the first place, while output may be massive, market research on readership may not be so sophisticated. Even after two decades of violent conflict Northern Ireland rates sparse mention in general VIth form or undergraduate textbooks concerned with contemporary British history and politics. It is as if authors consider it alien to the British political experience. This is rather curious if only because the problem has had a debilitating effect on the political process. One thinks of the obvious, such as the huge security operations which attend every party conference in the aftermath of the attempt to assassinate the prime minister and most of her cabinet at Brighton in 1984. One could add the financial drain which Northern Ireland continues to impose on the Exchequer, the introduction of Draconian legislation which casts doubt on the quality of British democracy and the embarrassment within the international community attached to the conduct of Northern Irish business. Others could be added. In short, Northern Ireland continues to be a major problem on the political agenda, and yet there still seems to be a lack of knowledge in Britain about the conflict.

Secondly, we should heed E. H. Carr's remark that the date of publication can be more revealing than the name of the author on the title page. This publication is acutely conscious of the significance of the Anglo-Irish Agreement of 1985. Clearly, it is much too early to make any proper historical judgement on the place of the Agreement in the tangled affairs of the Anglo-Irish process, but this much can be said: it has changed the nature of the debate within Northern Ireland and has changed the power relationships as a result. The unionist community feels bereft of friends. Indeed, it feels a sense of great betrayal on the part of the sovereign power. Given the unionists' seemingly absolute dominance from 1921 to 1972, and their relative confidence that they could count on an acceptable minimal support in Great Britain, particularly from a Conservative government, it is difficult to convey the psychological damage done since 1972 to their self-confidence and their ability to negotiate a new arrangement within Northern Ireland with the minority community. That, it might be said, is a matter peculiar to the people of Northern Ireland. But the implications of the 1985 Agreement are such that a much greater onus is placed on the British political process than heretofore. Northern Ireland may be treated as a sideshow by the daily tabloids but cabinet ministers know that it is a matter which can raise its ugly head at any time at their weekly meetings. In other words, while it may not be a matter of continuing debate in academia or the pub, it is a very serious issue in the conduct of every government. This book hopes to draw the salient issues to the attention of a wider audience in the hope that it will stimulate a more informed debate.

We have attempted to provide a thematic investigation of Northern Ireland rather than a purely chronological narrative of the Troubles. The latter can be found in a wide variety of publications, some of which are listed at the end. In chapter 1, however, we discuss the main lines of political developments in the province with particular emphasis on the events of 1968–9, 1974 and since the Anglo-Irish Agreement. Chapter 2 comprises a social and economic analysis, while nationalist and unionist politics – and their relationship with paramilitary activity – are covered in the next two chapters. Security challenges and responses are investigated in chapter 5 and international aspects, especially the burgeoning Anglo-Irish dimension and US involvement, are treated in chapter 6. We conclude with a review of proposed 'solutions' and the realistically available policy options.

In writing about Northern Ireland we are sharply aware that language, like everything else in Ireland, has a political dimension. In this respect sensitivity is a key element. The people of Northern Ireland have highly tuned political antennae. Words, accents, even vowels and consonants can convey political flavour. Rather than qualify every sentence in the text, we consider it prudent to announce at the outset that the following clusters will be used without attempting to convey anything sinister or offensive: catholic/nationalist/republican; protestant/unionist/loyalist; Derry/Londonderry (although the particularly sensitive might assert that they should appear in the opposite order); the Irish Republic/Eire/the Republic of Ireland/the South (and for the mathematically inclined 'the twenty-six counties'); similarly Ulster/Northern Ireland/the North/the six counties. All of these can impart a political message which it would be foolhardy to ignore. We try to avoid that trap by being specific in places, but we know that we cannot always get it absolutely right. In any case, to employ these terms without being conscious of their frequently intense political meaning might suggest some form of indifference about the nature of the problem. We hope we are not guilty.

Finally there is the issue of perspective. It takes two forms. One is to state bluntly that it is meaningless to examine developments inside Northern Ireland exclusively since 1968. Our sense of history is profound *and* shallow. Hence, while we are concerned with events since 1968, references to past happenings will be both frequent and necessary. 'History' can be a weapon. The second form concerns the sense of locality and of the individual within that locality, even what some people dismiss disparagingly as 'parochialism'. Undoubtedly it is the case that the level of violent incidents is diminishing, and that the population has become more 'case-hardened'. There are those who refer to the greater incidence of deaths through traffic accidents as if that excused the enormous waste of life through political violence. If nothing else, it is worth while reminding ourselves that the Troubles have not departed, that paramilitarism continues to be a way of life, and that each violent death not only diminishes all of us, but adds to our sense of hate or despair. Both emotions can fuel further violence.

As an afterword there is need for a health warning: all facts in a volatile political situation speak only for themselves when someone gives them the floor. It is the historian who sets the context: others might set different contexts from that which we have chosen, and it is important to remember that virtually every action and every utterance in Northern Ireland can be invested with at least two interpretations.

Jordanstown, county Antrim
September 1987

2 The Northern Ireland Political Landscape

Northern Ireland entered British political consciousness in the summer and autumn of 1968 when there were disturbances in the province following demonstrations sponsored by the Northern Ireland Civil Rights Association (NICRA). NICRA was a broadly based organization in which nationalists, liberal unionists, trade-union activists and other sympathetic parties had joined to press for reform of Northern Ireland's political system. Among their demands was the establishment of 'one-man-one-vote' in local government elections to replace the antiquated businessmen's and ratepayer's franchise which favoured the generally better-off protestant community. They also wanted to sweep away the gerrymandering of local-government boundaries which ensured the unionist domination of many local councils. In Londonderry County Borough in 1967, for example, 14,429 catholic voters (62 per cent of the total) out of 23,210 were able to elect only eight non-unionist councillors out of a total corporation of twenty. Another grievance lay in the discriminatory allocation of public housing. In Dungannon, county Tyrone (an area with a catholic majority), from 1945 to 1968 the local unionist council had allocated nearly three-quarters of the publicly built housing to protestants. It was no accident that the province's first civil rights march was held in the Dungannon area on 24 August 1968.

Although this march passed off peacefully, the second major demonstration, held in Derry on 5 October, was met by a strong contingent of Royal Ulster Constabulary (RUC) ordered in by the Minister of Home Affairs. The march ended with violent clashes and there was rioting throughout the catholic Bogside area of the city during the night that followed. In the autumn, further demonstrations – some which similarly ended in violence – marked the growing vigour of the civil rights movement, which was swelled especially by liberal and radical students from Queen's University in Belfast, attracted by the idealism of the cause and the opportunity it apparently presented for the introduction of 'real' politics in the province in place of the existing tired procedures of sectarian power-broking. NICRA and the student-led 'People's Democracy' (PD) drew inspiration from the contemporary American civil rights movement and also the wave of student unrest which swept across the world in 1968. At the turn of the year a PD march, consciously modelled on Martin Luther King's march from Selma to Montgomery, Alabama, in 1965, set out from Belfast to Derry. But a few miles short of Londonderry on the final day of their march the students were violently attacked by a mob of protestants, including a number of off-duty 'B-Specials', members of the exclusively protestant part-time auxiliary police. Again the Bogside erupted into violence with protestant rioters and some police joining in attacks on the catholics.

Faced with the apparently inexorable escalation of violence, and pressed for action by London, Captain Terence O'Neill, the well-meaning liberal who had been prime minister of the province since 1963, announced a package of reforms which to a very great extent met the original demands of NICRA. But within the unionist community such concessions generated unease and smacked of weakness in the face of violent challenge. Ian Paisley, the extreme evangelical cleric who had for some years been warning of the moral dangers of liberalism in general, caught the mood of many worried unionists when he accused O'Neill of traitorous behaviour. O'Neill, in any case, was not in the same mould as his predecessors. He did not appear to be as deeply rooted in the traditions of the protestant Orange Order and he lacked the common touch, an essential prerequisite in a tightly-knit community. Above all, he was a man with a mission, an innovator who wanted to prepare Northern Ireland for the late twentieth century and its place in the affluent sun. To achieve this a staid and conservative society needed to be shaken up. Besides, the governance of the province was coming under closer scrutiny from Great Britain. Labour, in power since 1964 under Harold Wilson, had little in common with unionism and resented the fact that at a time when Labour had a paper-thin majority Unionist MPs at Westminster voted with the Conservative opposition on matters of no direct concern to Northern Ireland. A backbench pressure group, the Campaign for Democracy in Ulster (CDU), paid close attention to the minority's complaints of discrimination. It had little difficulty in persuading Wilson to put pressure on O'Neill. In any event, the latter may have welcomed Wilson's insistence on reform since it enabled him to unleash an Ulster technocratic version of the 'white heat of the scientific revolution'.

O'Neill's modernization programme had a profound effect within his own community. He attempted to move the levers of power back to the 'centre' at Stormont (where the province's parliament sat) in a society which prided itself on decentralization, on strong local government and on a people who had a clear sense of their own autonomy. Many of them resented notions of centralized planning because it was being imposed by a faceless bureaucracy and was removing what little vestiges of power they felt still remained at local level. Hence Unionist Party revolts in 1966 and 1967 had been as much about the style of O'Neill's leadership as they were with the concessions he appeared to be making to the minority.

As it happened O'Neill's concessions were largely symbolic, if not cosmetic, but they did whet the appetite of the minority's leaders who were much defter than their unionist counterparts in the skills of public relations. Following the election of the Republican Labour candidate, Gerry Fitt, to Westminster in 1966, the minority had a powerful advocate who found a willing audience on the Labour back benches. The result was the introduction of a (muted) reform programme by the Northern Ireland prime minister which angered his more reactionary colleagues and disappointed civil rights activists. In attempting to push through his programme, Captain O'Neill lost four of his cabinet ministers who disagreed with the pace of reform. In response, he called a general election for February 1969 – 'Ulster at the Crossroads' – with the promise that if elected he would introduce universal suffrage at local-government level.

O'Neill won, but with a reduced majority and a serious rupture in his party. The impact of that split is still being played out in the unionist community. The impact on the nationalist minority was equally traumatic. The unionist electorate was presented with the opportunity to decide between thirty-nine O'Neill Unionists, seventeen anti-O'Neill Unionists and five Protestant Unionists. It chose twenty-two O'Neillites and eleven anti-O'Neillites. Whereas the Protestant Unionists were unsuccessful on this occasion, their leader, Ian Paisley, performed creditably and his party warmed to the electoral process: within four months he and his deputy were returned to Stormont in by-elections caused by the resignation of Terence O'Neill and a prominent backbencher, Richard Ferguson. Ferguson and others from liberal wing of the Unionist Party later gave support for the bi-communal moderate Alliance Party formed in April 1970. The significance of the February 1969 election for the minority was the challenge to the major opposition Nationalist Party from civil rights activists. Three of them, including John Hume, were elected and they proved to be the nucleus of the Social Democratic and Labour Party (SDLP) formed in August 1970, the most successful nationalist party in the history of Northern Ireland to date. If nothing else, the O'Neill general election radically altered the contours of the political landscape.

O'Neill's departure was assisted by explosions at electrical power installations and a water pipeline in March and April 1969, the handiwork of protestant extremists anxious to help him on his way. His political manner had suggested a more sedate age but his policies had induced a more raucous style of political behaviour. The civil rights campaign, largely based on extraparliamentary activity, produced a strong reaction from a section of the majority community which objected to what it considered a policy of appeasement orchestrated by an alien Labour government in London and carried out by its

O'Neillite puppets. Frequent sectarian clashes became the order of the day. Such activity was not unknown in Northern Ireland, but its intensity and consistency after October 1968 gave genuine cause for alarm in Britain where this sort of thing was not expected within the United Kingdom in the late twentieth century.

Westminster and Whitehall's ignorance and innocence were early casualties of 'the Troubles'. Civil servants sent from London to oversee the reform programme took some time to familiarize themselves with the idiosyncracies of the local scene. In particular they worked under the mistaken assumption that they were dealing with a political culture which would be as familiar to them as Surrey or Yorkshire. They were to make the same error as Terence O'Neill in assuming that there were technocratic answers to constitutional conundrums. More importantly, they were unaware of the traditional ambivalence to the political process present in both communities. Obviously they were conscious of the recurring street violence and they knew enough history to fear the potential for IRA resurgence. They believed that, at one level, violent political conflict could be resolved by social change. Those who could not be persuaded to enjoy the fruits of a reform programme would constitute a tiny romantic movement which would inevitably wither away. The problem with this approach was that it was based on a rationale which took little account of the longevity and intensity of the quarrel.

This intensity was soon abundantly obvious when very serious violence broke out in the summer of 1969. Faced with quickly escalating riots in Derry and Belfast, where protestant mobs launched savage attacks on catholic areas of west Belfast, the RUC proved unable to cope and O'Neill's successor as prime minister, Major James Chichester-Clark, asked London for the British army to be deployed on the streets. This was a crucial development. It marked a qualitative change in the nature of the crisis with London becoming more directly involved in the management of the problem. No longer could the violence be dismissed as merely an internal Northern Irish affair. The security arrangements made in the early days, moreover, reflected the haphazard and *ad hoc* nature of British decision-making towards the province. The rapid deployment of the British army in a 'peacekeeping' role on 15 August 1969 was ordered by London to meet an immediate and urgent crisis. As is often the case in such circumstances, little thought seems to have been given to the long-term implications. In particular, the precise relationship between the military and the police remained unclear. Four days after the troops had been sent in, a joint meeting of representatives from the United Kingdom and Northern Ireland governments at 10 Downing Street, London, agreed that the army General-Officer-Commanding (GOC) would assume 'overall responsibility for security operations'. While remaining answerable 'directly to the Ministry of Defence' (in London), he was to 'work in the closest co-operation with the Northern Ireland Government' and the head of the Royal Ulster Constabulary. For 'normal police duties outside the field of security', the RUC would remain under the direct administration of the Northern Ireland government.

The security chiefs were also subject to local political pressure. The GOC and Chief Constable were both members of a joint security committee which handled general questions of security policy. Chaired by the Northern Ireland Minister of Home Affairs, the committee provided a mechanism for local political and civil service views to be expressed on security matters. On occasions these views vigorously challenged the GOC's opinions. From the start, however, there were difficulties, especially since the problem, and hence the response, was seen rather differently by each interested party. The Northern Ireland government, for example, tended to view the unrest as an IRA-fomented challenge to the state as a whole, while some on the military side believed that both the Belfast administration and the local police themselves had contributed directly to the seriousness of the violence. Thus the central direction of the security effort was flawed. In London the high-level cabinet committee on Northern Ireland did little in the way of policy-making after August 1969. In the words of one of its members it was 'mainly concerned with sorting out the endless disputes between Freeland [the GOC] and the police or between the Ministry of Defence and the Home Office'. One early police–army difference concerned their respective spheres of responsibility as laid down after the Downing Street meeting of 19 August. This was in any case not very satisfactory, since the term 'security operations' was never clearly defined. When Sir Arthur Young, of the City of London Police, was appointed Chief Constable of the RUC in October 1969 he insisted, on the threat of resignation, that the GOC's role be restricted merely to 'co-ordinate' army and police.

There was equal, and growing, uncertainty on the political side. No one was quite sure who was ultimately in charge. London, understandably anxious to keep the whole mess at arm's length, was keen to work through the existing government of Northern Ireland while asserting (if not actually implementing) the sovereignty of the Westminster parliament. This was clearly set out in the 'Downing Street Declaration' of 19 August 1969 which also sought to reassure unionists by reaffirming 'the clear pledges made by successive United Kingdom Governments that Northern Ireland should not cease to be a part of the United Kingdom without the consent of the people of Northern Ireland'. 'The border', it bluntly added, 'is not an issue'. Since 1969, in fact, the British government's policy towards Northern Ireland has been to subcontract the day-to-day administration of the province on to some local body, while laying down certain minimum political requirements and retaining ultimate control of security.

It was over security matters that the Stormont system finally collapsed. Between the summer of 1969 and the resignation of the Northern Ireland government (by this stage under Brian Faulkner) in March 1972, London steadily expanded its control over security policy. The early reforms insisted upon in 1969 had begun to dismantle the traditional Northern Ireland security apparatus. The B-Specials were disbanded and replaced by the Ulster Defence Regiment (UDR), which although locally raised and mostly part-time was an integral part of the army and thus controlled from London. There was also a major reform of the RUC, which was disarmed, demilitarized and put under the command of an English policeman, Sir Arthur Young, although notably one with colonial experience. While the police were undergoing this process and recovering from the disasters of 1969, the army assumed the chief role of keeping the peace, yet Stormont still retained a major share in policy-making. In 1970–1, for example, the Northern Ireland government pressed London strongly for the introduction of internment without trial, but when the measure was introduced in August 1971 it turned out to be an unmitigated disaster which was followed by an increase in the level of unrest. The apparently uncontrollable spiral of violence in 1971–2 eventually led Edward Heath to transfer full responsibility for law and order to Westminster. In response Faulkner resigned and direct rule was established with William Whitelaw appointed the first Secretary of State for Northern Ireland.

Whitelaw's great achievement while responsible for Northern Ireland affairs was the creation of the powersharing executive, the most successful of the British political initiatives within the province so far. This initiative, like all others, sought to square the circle of meeting nationalist aspirations without fatally alienating the unionists. The executive, which drew together a group of comparatively moderate unionists, under Brian Faulkner (who became chief executive), the SDLP and the Alliance Party, took office on 1 January 1974 but lasted for just five months. Although candidates favouring powersharing had secured a comfortable majority (fifty out of seventy-eight) in the elections for a local assembly in June 1973, twenty-eight of the fifty unionists returned were resolutely opposed to the idea. In the general election to Westminster in February 1974, moreover, before the executive had had time to prove itself, eleven out of the twelve Northern Irish seats were won by anti-powersharing unionists fighting together in the United Ulster Unionist Council (UUUC) which secured 51 per cent of the poll. The UUUC claimed that the result was a clear vote of no confidence in Faulkner's executive. Apart from the repugnant notion of sharing power with 'disloyal' members of the minority community, the UUUC took particular exception to the establishment of a Council of Ireland which was supposed to consider matters of common interest, North and South, and to give Dublin a formal – if only consultative – role in the political process.

The UUUC alone did not destroy the executive, but its electoral success legitimized the loyalist protest – the Ulster Workers' Council (UWC) strike of May 1974 – which did. With a combination of disciplined industrial action and open intimidation, the UWC brought the province to a virtual stand-still. This extraparliamentary action was supported by the leading anti-powersharing politicians, such as Ian Paisley and the former Unionist cabinet minister, William Craig, but the real strength of the strike lay with protestant paramilitary organizations: the Ulster Defence Association (UDA), the Ulster Volunteer Force, the Ulster Special Constabulary Association and the Orange Volunteers. The Secretary of State (Merlyn Rees since the February Westminster election) was apparently unwilling to do anything to counter the power of these groups beyond mouthing the usual sort of pious plati-tudes. Harold Wilson made a broadcast to Northern Ireland in which he called the loyalist strikers 'thugs and bullies' who were 'sponging on British democracy', but he did nothing to match their *force majeure*. British trades-union leaders led an abortive 'back-to-work' march and the security forces remained on the sidelines until near the end of the strike when some moves were begun to mitigate the impact of the stoppage. The UWC's main power lay in its control of the electricity generating industry. The manual workers – mostly protestant – walked out and the white-collar staff, who might have kept a reasonable supply going for at least a limited period, were intimidated into running the system down. As the power cuts got longer and longer the Unionist members of the executive resigned and powersharing collapsed.

The events of May 1974 are crucial to an understanding of the loyalist reaction to the Anglo-Irish Agreement of November 1985. Drawing on the experience of 1974 (and, indeed, on 1912–21 when Irish Home Rule was successfully resisted in Ulster) the loyalist community believed it could literally pull the plug on any political arrangement constructed by the

British government which did not suit them. Loyalist reaction to the powersharing executive, moreover, was not only a matter of strikes and demonstrations. During the UWC stoppage car bombs believed to have been planted by protestant extremists exploded in Dublin and Monaghan in the Republic, killing twenty-seven people. Loyalist terrorists, though much less active than republican, have also played a significant role in the Troubles, especially at times of political uncertainty – 1969, 1974 or in the aftermath of the Anglo-Irish Agreement.

After the fall of the powersharing executive, the 1970s can be seen as a period of political stalemate. While the British government remained wedded to the notion of powersharing, it was unable to persuade the Northern Ireland political parties to agree to implement such an arrangement. A Constitutional Convention set up in May 1975 was dominated by loyalist intransigents who formulated a scheme which effectively called for the restoration of the Stormont system and specifically rejected powersharing at cabinet level. London refused to accept this proposal and dissolved the Convention in March 1976. Both Roy Mason (Secretary of State 1976–9) and Humphry Atkins (1979–81) introduced 'initiatives' which led to inconclusive talks with the local political parties. In each case the refusal of unionists to contemplate full powersharing proved to be an insuperable stumbling-block. And as successive British attempts to secure an internal settlement failed, the SDLP increasingly began to look south for a way out of the imbroglio.

So, in fact, did London. An important development of British policy towards Northern Ireland has been the growing belief in London that the Irish government must play a central part in *any* resolution of the conflict. Anglo-Irish relations were poor, to say the least, in the early 1970s. The apparent inability of the British government to control the escalating violence was widely criticized in the Republic. The events of 'Bloody Sunday', 30 January 1972, when British soldiers shot dead thirteen unarmed men during a demonstration in Derry, particularly inflamed sections of Southern opinion. An angry crowd marched on the British Embassy in Dublin and burnt it down.

But the Northern troubles also posed a threat to the peace and stability of the Republic, and the possibility of both loyalist and republican violence spreading south of the border was shockingly brought home to Southerners by the bombs of May 1974, the assassination of Christopher Ewart-Biggs, the British Ambassador to the Republic, in July 1976, and the killing of Lord Mountbatten near his county Sligo holiday home in August 1979. Dublin's wish to secure a peaceful solution to the Northern conflict is underpinned by the growing economic burden of maintaining a heightened security effort and an appreciation of the challenge – largely irrelevant to the everyday concerns of the Republic – posed to the Southern political system by extreme republicanism.

Such considerations have led successive Irish governments to participate in a process which led to the Anglo-Irish Agreement of November 1985. This process began in May 1980 when Mrs Thatcher and Charles Haughey, the Irish Taoiseach (prime minister), reached agreement on 'new and close political co-operation'. A few days later the chief constable of the RUC and the Garda (Irish police) Commissioner met for the first time to discuss improved cross-border security arrangements. At the end of the year Thatcher and Haughey met again and agreed to establish Anglo-Irish studies on matters of common concern. In a significant phrase, the two prime ministers contemplated an examination of 'the totality of relationships within these islands'. The joint studies reported in November 1981 and recommended, among other things, the establishment of an 'Intergovernmental Council' of ministers to review Anglo-Irish policy towards Northern Ireland.

In 1981 and 1982, however, Anglo-Irish relations were at times very strained. Dublin was sharply critical of Mrs Thatcher's handling of the republican hunger strikes in 1981, and the 'H-block' campaign (named after the shape of the buildings in the Maze Prison) in support of the strikers was able to mobilize opinion in the Republic – so much so that two hunger strikers were elected to the Dail (Dublin parliament) in the general election of June 1981. In the spring of the following year Mr Haughey's criticism of British policy towards the

Argentine occupation of the Falklands led to a diplomatic estrangement with Mrs Thatcher which was not repaired until November 1983, a year after Garrett FitzGerald had succeeded Haughey as Taoiseach.

Meanwhile the British government once more turned its attention to the possibility of an internal solution in Northern Ireland. In the autumn of 1982 a new Assembly was established to which, it was hoped, responsibilities for local affairs could progressively be transferred from the Westminster-based Northern Ireland Office. This idea of 'rolling devolution' depended, however, on a measure of agreement – which did not emerge – between the main political parties. The SDLP, while fighting the elections for the Assembly, boycotted its meetings on the grounds that a purely internal settlement was no longer viable. Without SDLP participation the initiative could never amount to much. The unionist parties and Alliance co-operated in developing some scrutinizing functions for the Assembly, but no scheme for powersharing which could include the SDLP was agreed. In the absence of any such proposal the Assembly lapsed into no more than an expensive and futile talking-shop. It was finally dissolved on 23 June 1986.

The re-establishment of friendly relations between Dublin and London which Garret FitzGerald earnestly desired was marked by the summit meeting with the British prime minister in November 1983, after which the intergovernmental council commenced operating. Between November 1983 and March 1985 the council met thirty times and paved the way for the Anglo-Irish Agreement signed at Hillsborough Castle, county Down, on 15 November 1985 (see Appendix for the full text of the Agreement). By formalizing the joint efforts of the British and Irish governments to secure reconciliation in Northern Ireland, the Agreement provided unequivocal acceptance that the problem was a joint one. In order to reassure the Northern unionists, Article 1 contained the two governments' affirmation 'that any change in the status of Northern Ireland would only come about with the consent of a majority of the people of Northern Ireland'. But, to the unionists' horror, Dublin was given a consultative role as of right regarding policy in the

North. Within the framework of the intergovernmental council, Article 2 provided that an intergovernmental conference would be convened regularly to consider '(i) political matters; (ii) security and related matters; (iii) legal matters, including the administration of justice; (iv) the promotion of cross-border co-operation'. The bulk of the Agreement outlined what was to be the role of the conference with special reference to these four matters. It was to be serviced by a secretariat composed of senior officials from London and Dublin based at Maryfield, outside Belfast. The secretariat was to act as a channel of communication between the governments, but not as a decision-making body.

The Agreement received a very wide welcome in Britain, Ireland and internationally. The House of Commons ratified it with an overwhelming majority of 426. In the Dail the vote was much closer – 88 to 75 – although still clearly in favour. The Agreement was registered with the United Nations and favourably received by President Reagan and the US Congress. International goodwill also came from all major West European states, the EEC, and from Canada, Australia and New Zealand. The importance of the international dimension was recognized in the Agreement itself. Article 10(a) saw the potential of promoting economic and social development to regenerate a depressed local economy by considering 'the possibility of international support'. The US, Canada and New Zealand contributed to an International Fund and, although the sums donated were relatively small (the US giving $120 million over three years), the contributions have considerable symbolic significance as an indication of international goodwill.

Apart from the guarantee that the constitutional status of Northern Ireland would not be altered without the consent of the population, the framers of the Agreement hoped to deflect unionist opposition by building in considerable flexibility – some would say 'ambiguity' – to the operation of the conference. The intention was to make the conference unboycottable, if not impervious to criticism. In the first instance local politicians were not to be involved in its workings. Yet Articles 4(b), 5(c) and 10(b) were designed to act as catalysts towards achieving powersharing devolution within the province in place of an *enhanced* role for the conference.

But the unionists responded to the Agreement with very bitter and sustained opposition. 'We are going to be delivered, bound and trussed like a turkey ready for the oven, from one nation to another nation', declared James Molyneaux, the leader of the Ulster Unionist Party (UUP), to a special sitting of the Northern Ireland Assembly the day after the Agreement had been signed. A massive loyalist demonstration on 23 November 1985 brought Belfast city centre to a standstill when a crowd, estimated at between 50,000 and 100,000 (over 10 per cent of the *entire* protestant population), proclaimed its profound opposition to the measure. A *Sunday Times* opinion poll the following day found 49 per cent of protestants opposed to the Agreement with only 14 per cent in favour. Beyond the loyalist gut reaction against the deal, however, the unionist community has been unable to devise any clear and satisfactory strategy to destroy, or even amend, the Agreement. While James Moly-neaux and the Democratic Unionist Party (DUP) leader Ian Paisley attempted to control and lead reaction through street demonstrations, Westminster and local-government boycotts, and a muted campaign of civil disobedience, some of the secondary leadership moved off on disparate paths.

Some toyed with forms of independence, while others, such as the Campaign for Equal Citizenship, pressed for the integration of Northern Ireland within the United Kingdom generally. They argued that if the 'national' parties organized in the province, as elsewhere in the UK, this would enable the removal of sectarianism from local politics. The leader of this group, Robert McCartney, a prominent unionist QC, stood on an 'equal citizenship' ticket in the June 1987 Westminster general election and polled 14,467 votes in the North Down constituency. In the same election, however, one of the leading integrationists, Enoch Powell, lost his seat to the SDLP. An alternative option was mapped out by the Charter Group, led by the former Stormont cabinet minister Harry West, which opposed administrative devolution and sought regional autonomy. Of the two main unionist parties, the DUP was more resolute in its opposition to the Agreement and adopted a more militant line which set the tone for its extraparliamentary campaign, much of it to the embarrassment of the UUP. Violence, for example, occurred outside Maryfield on 11 December 1985 and 4 January 1986, in various parts of the province following a 'day of action' on 3 March 1986 and in Portadown in March and July. On the first anniversary of the signing of the Agreement two people died and seventy were injured following loyalist demonstrations. In Belfast city centre over seventy shops were damaged, and some looted, after a mass protest around the city hall. Supporters of the UUP, more traditionally conservative and law-abiding than their DUP colleagues, have been disturbed by the violence accompanying opposition to the Agreement, especially attacks on the RUC. The level of violence has generally increased in the post-Agreement period. Fatal casualties rose by 21 per cent in 1986, and the total for the whole year had already been exceeded by the end of August 1987. Much of the increase was due to a sharp rise in loyalist paramilitarism in its campaign against the Agreement. Equally disturbing was the rise in the level of intimidation: at the end of 1986 the Housing Executive reported that it had dealt with 1,118 cases of families driven from their homes, almost all the result of loyalist paramilitaries attacking the houses of catholics or members of the RUC. L 1956/941.605

By mid-1987 explicit unionist opposition to the Anglo-Irish Agreement had somewhat declined. Unionist local councils were returning to normal activity. High hopes had been entertained that the United Kingdom general election in June might produce a 'hung' parliament in which the unionist MPs (as in 1977–9) could exert a disproportionate influence. Mrs Thatcher's clear victory, however, left the unionists with no specific policy beyond opposition to the Agreement. This has unsettled many unionist supporters and there is evidence of continuing rifts within the unionist family, including resignations of some younger active members of both parties who have apparently been frustrated by the negativism of party policy. Under the Anglo-Irish Agreement (Article 11) there has to be a review by November 1988 and it is clear that all sides are working towards this deadline. The government undoubtedly hopes that the unionists will in some way find themselves able to live within the framework established at Hillsborough, but as yet the unionist leadership has shown no sign of doing this. Ironically, unionist intransigence has helped to sustain nationalist support for the Agreement. While unionists object so strongly to the measure, many nationalists feel that it must have something to recommend it. But without further tangible benefits – especially in the administration of justice – nationalists may begin to look more critically at the arrangement.

3 A Place Apart

In 1976 the well-known Irish travel writer Dervla Murphy, who had published celebrated accounts of her bicycle journeys to India and other remote parts, toured Northern Ireland for the first time. The outcome of her visit was a brilliant and compassionate book, *A Place Apart*, which provides one of the best possible introductions to the communities and psychology of the North. Before her journey Dervla Murphy, who comes from county Waterford in the south-east corner of Ireland, had shared with many of her compatriots a fixed view of Northern Ireland as a peculiar place, mainly populated by irrational and violent people, which although lying within the island of Ireland is a very different and distinct locality. But Northern Ireland is a place apart not only in Ireland but also in the United Kingdom. Nearly seventy years of separate administration coupled with almost twenty years of communal unrest, moreover, have exacerbated these differences and enhanced its 'apartness'. Yet the north of Ireland has always had a particularity all of its own, in religious, social, economic and even national terms. It must also be borne in mind that Northern Ireland is an extremely parochial place and one result of the Troubles has been to make it more so. Matters of life and death have forced people to fall back on their own resources and to close ranks. The proximity both of the communities to each other and of politicians to the people they represent has enormously enhanced the primacy of specifically local issues and tragically reduced the capability of politicians of one tradition to empathize with their colleagues of the other.

The Northern Ireland conflict is frequently characterized as a religious one. In a technical sense this is not true. Although religious observance and churchgoing remain at a higher level in the province than in the rest of the United Kingdom, people in Northern Ireland are not fighting about theological points such as transubstantiation, predestination or papal infallibility. The leaders of the mainstream Christian denominations have consistently deplored the use of violence in the province and the frequent condemnation of violence by the catholic hierarchy, including the Pope during his visit to Ireland in 1979, make it absurd to suppose that members of the IRA, for example, are in any way expressing catholic *religious* opinion. Nevertheless religion remains a key social and political determinant in the province. It is not a question of religious belief but one of social and political identification. Put simply, most unionists are to be found in the protestant community and most nationalists in the catholic one. To a very great extent, and increasingly so since the Troubles began, catholics and protestants live in separate areas, they are educated apart and develop distinct cultural identities.

In general the self-perception of the protestant is one of 'British' nationality, loyalty to the British Crown and a commitment to the kinds of civil and political liberties established in Britain by the events of the seventeenth century, particularly the 'Glorious Revolution' of 1688. Although in Great Britain the political significance of the exclusively protestant nature of the British monarchy, as established in 1688, has largely disappeared, in Northern Ireland it remains a crucial component of the Ulster protestant's loyalty to the British Crown. The Ulster 'loyalist' is, above all, a protestant loyalist. For the catholic it is rather different. Irish nationality is combined with a history of national and religious subordination to 'English imperialism' and a heritage of the partially successful struggle for Irish freedom. For some catholics (although only a tiny minority of the total) the IRA campaign is simply the contemporary expression of that continuing battle.

Given that political attitudes and religious identification roughly coincide, then the communal 'numbers game' in

Northern Ireland assumes a very great importance. Successive guarantees by the British government that the constitutional status of Northern Ireland can be changed only with the agreement of a majority of the population, and the similar assurance contained in the Anglo-Irish Agreement, mean that the relative size of the two communities – and potential changes therein – is of vital significance. In the mid-1980s the population of Northern Ireland is about 1.55 million of which approximately 40 per cent are catholic. This proportion has increased over the years. In the mid-1920s just over one-third of the population (33.7 per cent) was catholic. Geographically, catholics are concentrated in the south and west of the province, and in west Belfast. Of the six counties which comprise Northern Ireland, there is a very substantial non-catholic majority of four or five to one in Antrim and Down. In Belfast the proportion is about two to one, while in the counties of Londonderry and Armagh non-catholics are in a small majority. In Fermanagh and Tyrone, however, catholics have a small majority.

Although catholic birthrates and family size are significantly higher than non-catholic, traditionally high rates of catholic emigration have restricted the growth of that community. Nevertheless, it has been calculated that between 1961 and 1981 the catholic population grew ten times faster than the non-catholic. Whether this trend will ineluctably continue until catholics achieve a numerical majority is of real political concern. What we can say is that, barring any apocalyptic – and highly unlikely – circumstance in which there is a major movement of protestants *out* of Northern Ireland, the erosion of the protestant majority will be a very long-term process. In the first place, over the past fifteen years the rate of growth in the catholic population has slowed down markedly. Secondly, the catholic community is not a homogeneous political unit and a proportion of it may be expected even in the present situation to assent to the maintenance of Northern Ireland within the United Kingdom.

The growth of the population as a whole has been limited by emigration from both communities. There was a net outflow of 110,000 people between 1971 and 1981, more than half of whom went to Great Britain. More recently the number of emigrants has fallen due to the world economic recession and the reduction of employment opportunities abroad. With the recession hitting Northern Ireland particularly hard, this has meant that the problem of unemployment in the province has been more than usually exacerbated in the 1980s, a factor which inevitably has repercussions for social and political harmony.

There is also some evidence that the balance of emigration between the Northern Ireland communities is changing with protestants now becoming more likely to leave the province than catholics. Apart from the political uncertainty, this reflects the greater ability of protestants in general to secure employment abroad. They are more likely to possess marketable skills and to have higher educational qualifications than catholics. There is also an emotional aspect. A catholic school-leaver with good A levels, brought up in a nationalist tradition, may prefer to go to an Irish university (North or South) than one elsewhere in the United Kingdom, while a 'British' protestant will have no such compunctions. It seems to be the case, moreover, that only a small percentage of those protestants who go 'across the water' to university ever return to live in the province. Such a social haemorrhage may in the long term have had an impact on the quality of leadership – of all kinds – available for the protestant community.

Education is an area of marked segregation between catholics and protestants in Northern Ireland. Early in its life the unionist government at Stormont introduced an education act aimed at establishing an essentially secular, publicly-funded system of primary education throughout the province. But there was such strong opposition from both the catholic and the protestant churches (who wished to retain control over education) that the government was obliged to drop the measure. Although the amended act asserted that the state education system should be non-sectarian, it also stipulated (as was the case elsewhere in the United Kingdom) that Christian religious education be included in the syllabus. To qualify for a full government subsidy, however, a school had to provide distinctively protestant 'Bible teaching'. In effect this meant that the state primary-education system was a protestant one. A similar state of affairs obtained after 1947 when the Northern Ireland government, following the British Butler Education Act of 1944, introduced free secondary education for all so long as they stayed within the state sector but still restricted the assistance available for the province's specifically denominational (mostly catholic) schools. Since the late 1960s, a series of changes begun under Captain O'Neill have increased government subsidies for denominational schools and the catholic sector is now much less disadvantaged than before. But at the primary and secondary levels most children in Northern Ireland are still educated in religiously segregated institutions. Teacher training is similarly divided and will remain so for the foreseeable future. A recent attempt to rationalize teacher-training provision and amalgamate the two catholic colleges with the non-denominational state establishment was successfully opposed by the catholic hierarchy. These educational divisions have considerable social repercussions although they are as much a product of a divided community as a cause.

The situation is much more satisfactory in further and higher education which is almost totally integrated. The 1946 Education Act provided for grant-aided university education which gave new opportunities especially to catholic students, and facilitated the growth of a catholic professional class which in turn played a significant role in the development of the civil rights movement. The government funding for education at all levels in Northern Ireland has been rather more generous than anything available in the Republic. It is, ironically, currently cheaper in terms of fees for Southern students to come to university in the North than to stay at home, since under EEC regulations the British government is obliged to charge all EEC nationals at the same rate as home students.

Since the end of the Second World War social policies in Northern Ireland have gone 'step by step' with those in Great Britain. The welfare reforms of the wartime coalition and the postwar Attlee government were matched by similar measures in the province. But since Northern Ireland could not afford to fund these developments out of its own exchequer, Westminster has had to provide an annual subvention. In this, of course, Northern Ireland is no different from any other poor part of the United Kingdom except that with a separate exchequer the Treasury subvention is easier to calculate than otherwise. In order to maintain the national parity of social services, for example, Scotland or the north-east of England require subsidies from the prosperous south-east. In 1985–6 the Treasury subvention to Northern Ireland amounted to some £1,500 million, over one-third of the total annual public expenditure. Although the gap today is less than it was in the 1950s and 1960s, public spending on education, hospitals, pensions and social services is higher in Northern Ireland than in the Republic, with the result that the province's 'apartness' from the rest of Ireland is amplified by social-welfare considerations.

In the past the north-east of Ireland was also very distinct in economic terms for it was the only part of the island fully to experience nineteenth-century industrialization comparable to that occurring in Great Britain. The development of factory-based textile (mostly linen) production, engineering concerns, and in Belfast a world-scale shipbuilding industry marked Ulster out from the rest of Ireland, which lacked the basic raw materials – coal and iron ore – for an industrial revolution. Easy sea communications here worked in Ulster's favour, with coal and iron efficiently and economically being supplied from north-west England and south-west Scotland. Much of the risk capital for industrial development in the province came from Great Britain, and the customers for Ulster's industrial products were also British. It was Glasgow and Liverpool concerns, not Dublin or Cork, who purchased the ships built by the great Belfast yard of Harland & Wolff. The emergence of large-scale Ulster resistance to Home Rule in the late nineteenth century came at a time when, as never before, the economic and commercial prosperity of the region seemed to depend on the maintenance of close political links with Great Britain.

Today, in much less prosperous times, Northern Ireland's economic survival also seems to depend on the continuance of the union. Ulster was one of the last parts of the United Kingdom to industrialize and it was among the first to begin to experience the economic decline which has afflicted much of the country's traditional industries. With a brief respite during the Second World War, Northern Ireland has suffered high levels of unemployment since the 1920s. In August 1987 unemployment, which during the 1980s has exceeded 20 per cent, stood at over 18 per cent, in comparison to the United Kingdom's average of 10 per cent. The old staple industries have greatly declined. Harland & Wolff, which had 26,000 employees in Belfast in 1945, employed fewer than 4,000 forty years later. Between 1960 and 1985 the total numbers employed in manufacturing industry fell by 82,000, or 45 per cent, half of which were lost between 1978 and 1985. Over the same seven-year period employment in the construction industry fell by 39 per cent, from 38,000 to 23,000.

The existence of long-term structural unemployment has serious social implications, and successive Northern Irish administrations have made great efforts to reduce it. Employment in traditional textile manufacturing, which fell by 23,000 in the 1960s when the linen industry was in steep decline, was partly replaced by 10,000 new jobs in an expanding man-made-fibres industry, attracted to the province in part by government incentives. But the oil crisis of the 1970s, which sharply pushed up raw-material costs for synthetic-textile manufacturers, the civil disorders and world over-capacity led to the closure of many factories. The provision of subsidies, purpose-built factories, interest-free loans and other assistance through the Industrial Development Board (IDB) and the Local Enterprise Development Unit remains a central part of the government's economic strategy. Harland & Wolff, for example, only survives with a substantial government subsidy, which amounted to £68 million in 1986. The government's efforts to attract foreign investment have met with mixed fortunes. The understandable anxiety of politicians and officials to secure major industrial projects has led to serious misjudgements, such as in the case of the De Lorean Motor Company which collapsed in 1982 leaving debts of over £100 million.

Many of the particular problems faced by Northern Ireland's manufacturers are illustrated by the experience of Short Brothers, the government-owned aircraft and missile builder which with 7,000 jobs is the largest single industrial employer in the province. Although it made a small profit in 1984–5, 'Shorts' has required substantial public subsidies for more than a decade to remain in business. Ironically, it has recently suffered from its considerable success in winning work. In 1985 it won a £125 million contract from the Royal Air Force to build 130 trainer aircraft. At the end of 1986 the Ministry of Defence placed a £225 million order for its Starstreak air-defence missile system. Shorts also does a lot of sub-contracting work, especially for Boeing, including that from a recent agreement to manufacture parts for the new Boeing 7J7 airliner. Yet in November 1986 the company chairman, Sir Philip Foreman, announced losses of £35 million. The company, he said, had taken on too much work and had 'lost control of manufacturing'. On the industrial side, however, the future for Shorts looks comparatively secure since its products are evidently in demand. The appalling social (and political) costs of the company failing – 7,000 redundancies would be catastrophic for the province – will ensure at the very least a sympathetic government attitude towards future subsidies.

But Shorts' problems have an important political dimension. The company's main factory is located in east Belfast – hard loyalist territory – and the workforce is over 90 per cent protestant, with a long tradition of militant unionism which it shares with the men at the neighbouring Harland & Wolff shipyard. Politics and religion frequently spill over into the workplace, with loyalist flags and banners being displayed annually during the summer 'marching season'. In 1986 there were additionally some attacks on catholic workers. The management moved quickly to prevent a recurrence and also insisted on the removal of the loyalist flags. This provoked an immediate strike by 2,000 of the company's employees, who were only persuaded to return after the management had stressed the company's 'Britishness' and promised to fly the Union Flag permanently over the factory. The loyalist flags, however, were not replaced.

In recent years the company as a whole has come under scrutiny for its recruitment practices. The management could, in part at least, be held responsible for the small number of catholics in the firm and was particularly vulnerable to criticism from the United States in this respect. Not only was Shorts a Boeing subcontractor, but the US Air Force has made major purchases of Shorts' Sherpa freighter and the Shorts 330 commuter passenger aircraft is used by a number of US airlines. In the USA a campaign led by American–Irish republican sympathizers – the Irish National Caucus – has been developing to take action against Northern Irish firms which are perceived as discriminating against the minority. Shorts are understandably anxious not to be boycotted by Boeing or potential US customers, but traditional employment patterns and the location of the factory make it difficult to make quick changes. The company intends to move some of its operations to part of the former De Lorean car plant in west Belfast, and 25 per cent of the apprentices recruited are now catholic. But such moves may in turn alarm loyalists who see catholics as embodying a direct economic threat to their status.

US pressure for change in this area has coalesced around the so-called MacBride principles, approved by Sean MacBride, an IRA leader between the wars, Irish Foreign Minister 1948–51 and later a senior United Nations diplomat who won the 1974 Nobel Peace Prize and the 1977 Lenin Peace Prize. These principles comprise a series of guidelines for equal-opportunity work practices, including increased job opportunities for 'under-represented religious groups in the workforce' (effectively catholics), adequate security for minority employees, the prohibition of provocative sectarian symbols from the workplace and the abolition of employment criteria based on religious affiliation. This campaign, which has been linked to one calling for disinvestment from South Africa, has met with some success in the United States, despite the strenuous opposition of the British government, the leader of the SDLP, John Hume, and the American government. Legislation has been adopted in New York, for example, preventing any state pension fund from investing in US companies in Northern Ireland which are judged to be guilty of discrimination. US investment is very important to the province. A number of major concerns, such as Ford, General Motors, the Hughes Tool Company and Du Pont Chemicals, have branches here and these companies are certainly susceptible to shareholder pressure back home.

Three main objections have been levied against the Mac-Bride principles. In the first place the positive discrimination in favour of catholics envisaged by the principles would be illegal under current Northern Ireland legislation. The Fair Employment Act 1976 made it unlawful for an employer to discriminate in the selection of an employee on the grounds of religious belief or political opinion. Secondly it has been asserted that the Mac-Bride principles present a deceptively and dangerously simple answer to a very complicated problem. Applied enthusiastically by distant external activists, whose motives may not always be limited merely to an improvement in employment practices, the principles take little account of the complexities of the situation in Northern Ireland and in the end may make it more difficult to arrive at a satisfactory internal resolution of the problem. In the third place the principles have been characterized as counter-productive. Their impact may be actually to curtail US investment in Northern Ireland and thus reduce job opportunities all round. This, indeed, is the main consideration underlying the SDLP's doubts about the principles.

Yet the problem of continuing catholic disadvantage is a very real one. Measured by a variety of social indices, the catholic community remains underprivileged in comparison with the protestant. Catholics are, in general, poorer, less well-educated and more likely to be unemployed than protestants. A recent survey (1987) of school-leavers showed that 45 per cent of protestants had full-time employment, as against 32 per cent of catholics. The areas of greatest unemployment tend to be in predominantly catholic districts in the south and west of the province. In Strabane, for example, male unemployment stands at over 50 per cent. Although there have been improvements in the position of employed catholics, these have occurred from a comparatively low base. Between the 1971 and 1981 censuses, for example, the number of catholics who were 'managers of large establishments' more than doubled, while the protestant figure increased by just over half. But in 1981 catholics still comprised only 18.5 per cent of the total in this category. An investigation by the Fair Employment Agency (established under the 1976 Act) of the Northern Ireland Civil Service, the province's largest single employer with 20,000 employees, found that the relative numbers of people from each community had changed significantly between 1980 and 1985. In 1980 protestants comprised 64.5 per cent of the service, a figure slightly above the protestant percentage of the whole community. In 1985, however, that proportion had fallen to 59 per cent. Over this period the number of catholics in the civil service had increased by over one-fifth. Despite this improvement, the representation of each community at different levels of the service remains asymmetrical. Catholics are most numerous in the lower grades, while in the most senior levels (senior principal and above) in 1985 they comprised just under 10 per cent.

Clearly there is much to be done. Despite the 1976 legislation and the existence of the Fair Employment Agency with a specific brief to promote equitable employment practices, change has occurred only very slowly, especially in the private sector. Realizing this, and also responding to the impact of the MacBride campaign, in September 1987 the government announced the introduction of a new code of practice to ensure that there is no discrimination in this area. The code recommends that employers advertise vacancies widely, rather than relying on word-of-mouth recruitment. It deplores the preferential treatment of existing employees' relatives, and urges the removal of qualifications or conditions of employment which are not job-related, such as service in the armed forces. Although the code is voluntary, the government intends to back it up with a system of 'contract compliance' which goes beyond anything contained in the MacBride principles. The government is pledged to refuse to do business with anyone who does not comply with the code and since it is far and away the largest employer and placer of contracts in the province, this represents a substantial sanction.

The 'apartness' of the Northern Irish communities in religious, social, educational, economic and even geographical terms is very deep-rooted indeed. Nearly twenty years of communal – frequently sectarian – violence has served to deepen many of the divisions. The Troubles have also tended to confirm a 'partition mentality', both north and south of the border. For unionists, republican terrorism has merely confirmed their fear and dislike of the South, a state of mind which emerged very clearly indeed in the near-hysterical reaction to the Anglo-Irish Agreement. Ironically, for many Southern people the troubles have also confirmed partition. Many parlour nationalists who formerly would have paid lip service to the ideal of a united Ireland now positively reject that option, since it would, they believe, destructively incorporate in any new Irish state a million embittered and dangerous protestants. There is a marked contrast between these partitionist attitudes and the perception of British and Irish politicians that the difficulties of Northern Ireland can only be mitigated by closer co-operation between London, Dublin and both communities in the North. While the people of Ireland, North and South, have apparently moved further apart, the governments which represent the national aspirations of the differing communities in these islands have moved closer together. Therein lies one of the many curious paradoxes of contemporary Northern Irish history.

4 Catholic Politics

After the establishment of Northern Ireland in 1921, catholics – the minority – were largely excluded from politics in that part of the island. The slow development of active catholic political representation, moreover, was inevitably influenced by the prevailing unionist domination of the province and the extent to which unionists themselves actually set the political agenda. Until 1969 all general elections had an unerring and deadening predictability. The reasons were simple. The first-past-the-post electoral system encouraged strong single-party government, and, in a polity in which religious affiliation was the chief voting determinant, the protestant majority voted overwhelmingly for the Unionist Party. There was little choice. The opposition parties were fragmented and frustrated, devoid of proper organization and lacking an attractive and positive programme. As often as not, seats were uncontested: from 1929 to 1969 inclusive 37.5 per cent of all seats went unopposed, and in a fifty-two-seat lower house Unionists never held fewer than thirty-two.

It was not that the Unionist Party displayed obvious electoral verve or that in government it was particularly dynamic. On the contrary, it threw up very few politicians of real calibre – unlike many MPs from Scotland and Wales, no Ulster Unionist at Westminster was of sufficient stature to find a place in the cabinet. Equally, the government of Northern Ireland was no better than mediocre during this period. If the ability to stamp one's authority on the whole community and to command its respect is the hallmark of good and successful government, then (as events after 1969 demonstrated) Unionist government did not pass muster. It perceived its role as looking after the interests of the majority community and it did little in the way of attempting to woo the minority. Its record in respect of the former was clearly good enough to ensure those predictable electoral results.

Unionist success was built on a combination of the politics of patronage and its recurrent attempts at raising the spectre of nationalist domination. In a society of limited resources, it could not always guarantee the good life for its own supporters, but it could (and did) frequently raise emotions. It has to be said that there were some grounds for invoking fear. After all, the unionist population, one million at most, shared the island with a nationalist majority. The minority of that majority, about 500,000 people, were considered as fifth columnists residing within the territory, and the remainder belonged to a hostile state which made irredentist claims on Northern Ireland. It was, and is, written into the (1937) Constitution of the Irish Republic:

Art. 2   The national territory consists of the whole island of Ireland, its islands and territorial seas.

Art. 3   Pending the re-integration of the national territory and without prejudice to the right of the Parliament and Government established by this Constitution to exercise jurisdiction over the whole of that territory, the laws enacted by that Parliament shall have the like area and extent of application as the laws of Saorstat Eireann [i.e. over the twenty-six counties only] and the like extra-territorial effect.

Unionists, moreover, were conscious of the physical threat posed by the IRA. That organization was implacable in its opposition to partition and was prepared to adopt any means to dismantle the border and impose Irish unity. Its campaign of violence in 1956–62, for example, claimed the lives of six policemen and eleven republican activists or sympathizers. That it was not more successful had much to do with its own incompetence and its failure to garner enough covert sympathy from the catholic minority, above all in Belfast.

In these circumstances 'eternal vigilance' was the watchword of the majority, and its style of government laid heavy emphasis on security and on the dire necessity of keeping the ship of state afloat. Radical policies in any shape or form were to be eschewed as Northern Ireland basked in its self-induced image as a peaceful but provincial backwater. The unionist tradition, thus, draws on a heritage of both confident supremacy, based on its majority position in Northern Ireland and its ability, as in 1912–21, to mobilize powerful allies in Westminster, and perpetual siege, with its precious protestant community (and state) under threat both from the disloyal minority within the province and the apparently priest-ridden Irish Republic. The events of 1969 and after merely confirmed to convinced unionists like Paisley and many others the error of O'Neill's absurd woolly liberalism and exposed the reality of the continued threat to the very existence of Northern Ireland.

The principal agency of that threat over the past seventeen years has been the Provisional IRA which self-consciously embodies a sense of continuity with Ireland's ancient martyrs. It is a commonplace that the Irish are too interested in history and that they invoke the ghosts of history to justify present actions. Hence in its very first public statement the Provisional Army Council (formed in January 1970) declared its allegiance to 'the 32 county Irish Republic *proclaimed at Easter 1916* established by the First Dail Eireann in 1919, over-thrown by force of arms in 1922 and suppressed to this day by the existing British-imposed six county and twenty-six county partition states'. The hunger strikes of 1980 and 1981 compounded this capacity to draw on symbols which reinforced the Provisionals' claim to be the authentic republicans to such an extent that Christ was invoked: 'No greater love hath a man than to lay down his life for his friends'. A similar thrust can be found in loyalist circles. In a distinguished history of loyalism, *Queen's Rebels*, David Miller traces a tradition of 'public banding', whereby the protestant people of Ulster relied on their own resources to defend themselves, from the seventeenth century up to and including the formation of the Ulster Volunteer Force (UVF) to resist the Third Home Rule Bill of 1912, and the 'B Specials' which were in existence from 1920 to 1969. If the Ulster Covenant of 1912 (a solemn declaration committing Ulster to the Union and loyalty to the Crown, signed by 471,414 persons) symbolizes the determination and aspirations of the loyalist people, then the 1916 Proclamation with its declaration of an Irish Republic fulfils the same role for republicans. Both of them use the same ominous phrase – 'all means necesary' – to delineate the lengths to which they are prepared to go.

In times of crisis (and Northern Ireland has never enjoyed a sustained period of normality) there is a tendency to resurrect ancestral heroes, who may provide overt support to each community's paramilitaries. Thus, in the period of great uncertainty following the signing of the Anglo-Irish Agreement, many protestants recalled the memories of Sir Edward Carson and Sir James Craig, the architects of Northern Ireland, and some have tried to emulate the organization of the original UVF. Similarly, the Provisionals have drawn on a republican heritage reaching back to Wolfe Tone in the late eighteenth century and since 1970 they have been able to masquerade as the protectors of the catholic minority. As election statistics will show, moreover, their political wing, Sinn Fein, has converted this into political clout.

This needs some explanation before we embark on an examination of electoral fortunes in the 1970s. It is not that the people of Northern Ireland are particularly amoral, although propagandists on both sides attempt to portray their adversaries in lurid terms. Rather than attempting a detailed analysis of the reasons for community support for paramilitaries, we shall refer briefly to the position of the Provisional movement. Already we have observed one reason for its tenacity – continuity. A group which can demonstrate lineage with ancient heroes starts with certain advantages, but these cannot be sustained unless that community perceives a threat to its values if not to its very existence.

The political environment in which the Provisionals operate offers another explanation. One reason given for embarking on the hunger strike which was to claim ten prisoners' lives in 1981 was 'to advance the Irish people's right for liberty'. This demand strikes a highly-tuned emotional chord among a section of the population which believes that partition of the island in 1921 was immoral and was achieved solely through the loyalist threat of violence. The only proper response was to reply in kind. In that respect the genesis of Provisionalism is interesting. The Provisional IRA was formed after the 'old' Official IRA split in December 1969. It draws its title from the proclamation of the provisional government of the Republic of Ireland at the start of the Easter Rising in 1916, and affirms that any government in Ireland will be 'provisional' until the final establishment of a thirty-two county republic. Believing in the ultimate unity of the people of Ireland and the essential geographical and political indivisibility of the island, its primary immediate objective is to secure the withdrawal (as republicans see it) of British forces from Northern Ireland. It was not simply another manifestation of armed republicanism. It was born following loyalist attacks on the catholic ghettoes of west Belfast in August 1969. Its personnel were the young people of those areas intent on defending themselves. The graffito of the time – 'IRA = I Ran Away' – captures the sense of despair felt by many residents who believed that the old IRA leadership was more intent on conducting seminars in Marxist theory rather than looking after their own. The new breed were more indigenous and more ruthless. They were the children of the ghetto and until the mid-1970s when the IRA reverted to cellular system they were organized on a neighbourhood basis.

Much of the Provisionals' success depended upon military and security insensitivity. Between 1971 and 1978 inclusive there were more than 300,000 house searches, most of which would have occurred in republican areas. Not all of these, by any means, would have been conducted sensitively, and they were widely viewed as forms of community assault. The political response to the Provisionals, moreover, was inconsistent. The dualism of British government policy towards the organization is well illustrated by the events of 1972. After the establishment of direct rule in March, it seemed that perhaps after all London might consider a major change in the province's constitutional status. The introduction in June of 'special category' status – effectively a political status for convicted terrorists – was correctly taken by the Provisionals as a sign that the British government might be prepared to parley with them, even against the advice of the government of the Republic. On 26 June the Provisionals called a ceasefire. Early in July secret talks were held in Paul Channon's house in London between the Secretary of State for Northern Ireland, William Whitelaw, and representatives of the Provisional leadership, including Sean Mac-Stiofain, the Chief of Staff, Martin McGuinness from Derry and Gerry Adams, who had been released from detention especially for the occasion. The talks came to nothing and the ceasefire was called off soon afterwards. The Provisionals presented to Whitelaw a list of fixed demands, which they apparently thought the Cabinet might consider. Among these was that the British government should declare its intention 'to withdraw all British forces from Irish soil' before the beginning of 1975. Whether the Provisionals' delegation really believed that the British might accede to their wishes, or whether the whole affair was no more than a propaganda exercise on their part, these absolutely fixed demands disabused Whitelaw and his colleagues of any pious hopes they may have had that they could negotiate as politicians with the Provisional leadership.

Since the summer of 1972 the government has avoided any similar direct high-level links with illegal paramilitary groups. In terms of the Provisionals, the government's policy remains the eradication of violence and the suppression of the organization. They have, however, retained hopes that the political wing of the movement – Provisional Sinn Fein (PSF) – which was legalized in 1974 might in some way be encouraged to wean republican activists away from violence. During another Provisional ceasefire in the spring of 1975 joint 'incident centres' were set up, manned by government officials and members of PSF. This ceasefire also collapsed with the British government's refusal to accept the Provisionals' *sine qua non* – the demand for 'Brits out'. With the success of PSF candidates in local council elections in the 1980s, and the election of

Gerry Adams as Westminster member for West Belfast, the Provisional leadership has maintained the so-called 'ballot paper in one hand and Armalite rifle in the other' strategy. This has not been without strains. At the Provisional Sinn Fein annual conference in November 1986 a group styling itself 'Republican Sinn Fein' broke away from the main organization after the conference had voted to take up any seats its candidates might win in the Dublin parliament. It remains to be seen how significant this new splinter group may be, and whether it will develop any armed wing.

Loyalist activity (and rhetoric) has contributed to republican success. The New Ireland Forum calculated that in the period from 1969 to mid-1983 loyalist paramilitary groups were responsible for 613 deaths. Of course they had also been involved in the UWC strike of 1974, the constitutional stoppage of 1977, the creation of the 'Third Force' in 1981, and of the Ulster Clubs movement in 1985. In short, paramilitaries feed off each other and their respective communities remain reluctant to abandon them to a (British) government whose credentials are dubious.

An examination of the genesis of loyalist paramilitarism would reveal the same pattern, although its ledger of violence is not of the same magnitude and its self-perception as a counter-terrorist organization has some validity. However, the national-ist retort that the security forces had traditionally looked after the interests of the protestant community underlines the complexity of the problem and the difficulties in pursuing a solely political path. Suffice it to say that community ambival-ence towards political violence is grounded in constitutional uncertainty, genuine communal fears and a history of instabi-lity. All of that must be appreciated before one tries to under-stand why the political process has faltered.

When Danny Morrison, Sinn Fein Director of Publicity, asserted at the 1981 conference that republicans had 'a ballot paper in one hand and an Armalite rifle in the other' he was reflecting the euphoria of an organization which believed that it had ceased to be a sect and had become a mass movement. A year later the same sentiment appeared in the Sinn Fein newspaper *An Phoblacht* in the run up to the Northern Ireland Assembly elections. 'The essence of republican struggle', it declared, 'must be in armed resistance coupled with popular opposition to the British presence. So, while not everyone can plant a bomb, everyone can plant a vote'. This displayed a cynicism based on the arrogance of a movement which believed that its time had come. It had some reason to support this belief, but such was the apprehension aroused by the Provisionals that the mainstream political parties set out to remove whatever ambivalence to violence existed in the community. That task fell largely on the SDLP.

Until the hunger strikes the SDLP had enjoyed a virtually unchallenged position within the catholic community. There were several reasons for this. The most obvious was that there was no competition. With the passing exception of the Irish Independence Party, formed in 1977 on the more militant policy of seeking British withdrawal, the SDLP had a clear run. The IIP secured 3.3 per cent of the vote in the 1979 general election and 3.9 per cent in the 1981 local government elections but faded thereafter when its vote swung over to Sinn Fein.

Secondly we need to look at the nature of the SDLP. It has been the most successful party to represent the minority since partition. Until its appearance, the opposition was noted for its lack of organization. Its chief flagship, the Nationalist Party, had contested elections without a party headquarters and without paid officials. Until November 1964 it did not even have a party programme, save the principle of dismantling Northern Ireland as a political entity in favour of Irish unity. The SDLP, on the other hand, was formed on the enthusiasm whipped up by civil rights victories with the ensuing unionist discomfort. It was formed, too, with a distinct ideology and a strong belief in organization. In the Northern Irish context two of the party's objectives were noteworthy: 'to organise and maintain in Northern Ireland a Socialist Party', and 'to promote the cause of Irish unity based on the consent of the majority of people in Northern Ireland'. The first of these was realized through its membership of the Socialist International and the Confederation of Socialist Parties of the European Community. But the political terrain in which it worked and the fundamental problems which it encountered made the SDLP an atypical member of the European Socialist movement and its socialist credentials are more cosmetic than real.

It was atypical in the Northern nationalist tradition as well in that it accepted the doctrine of consent if Irish unity was to be realized. Unlike the old Nationalist Party it had to cast its appeal well beyond the narrow confines of a permanent catholic minority, and that meant paying attention to such things as organization and electoral appeal. Rather than be a single-issue party, it had to become a 'catch-more' party. It could not expect to be a 'catch-all' party in that it appreciated that its ideology was antithetical to traditional unionists. Rather, it had to woo waverers. Unlike Sinn Fein it did not believe in the armed struggle, and it had to offer a programme of hope which would remove the minority from despair and the clutches of the gunmen.

We shall see from the voting figures that the SDLP has had mixed success in these objects, but that the quality of tenacity is one which has remained with it through adversity. Paradoxically, the party may have benefited from lack of electoral success. With the exception of the short period January–May 1974, when it was in office as part of the powersharing administration, it has been consigned to a political limbo. Its republican opponents have been able to proclaim that this demonstrates that the minority cannot expect fair play inside the 'gerrymandered statelet' and that Northern Ireland is irreformable. If the SDLP continues – or so the propaganda would have it – it is because its members are unprincipled and are prepared to sell their nationalist souls for a mess of partitionist, powersharing pottage. To remain in the business of influencing the political debate, therefore, the SDLP has had to change its tactics to meet the twin challenges posed by the adversity of the internal electoral system and the seductive simplicity of 'the Armalite rifle and the ballot box'.

All of this has had an energizing effect on the party. The engineered collapse of the powersharing executive in 1974 and the subsequent refusal of the unionist parties to contemplate any form of powersharing acceptable to the British government has induced the SDLP to alter its strategy to include an enhanced role for Dublin in the political process. The culmination of this strategy is to be seen in the Anglo-Irish Agreement with its tacit 'internationalization' of the Northern Ireland problem and its short-term neutralization of the unionist veto. The architect of the new policy, John Hume (leader of the party since 1979) spelt it out in 1979 in an article for the prestigious American journal *Foreign Affairs* when he asserted that London and Dublin would have to act together in 'a positive and decisive initiative' which would remove any 'unconditional guarantees for any section of the northern community', and that the whole community must be made to realize that there are no simple solutions but only a process that will lead to a solution. In other words he was asserting the primacy of the political and the fundamental responsibilities of the two sovereign states.

This strategy unfolded through the Anglo-Irish process, beginning with a summit meeting in May 1980 and including other developments such as the report on the situation in Northern Ireland drawn up on behalf of the Political Affairs Committee of the European Parliament by Neils Haagerup and tabled on 2 March 1984. In the domestic domain the strategy enabled the party to keep its head above water as it came under increasing electoral pressure from Sinn Fein and equal pressure from the Secretary of State, James Prior, who was intent on making one last move towards a purely internal settlement when he created his Northern Ireland Assembly in October 1982. The SDLP fought that election on a policy of boycotting the Assembly, a policy incidentally also espoused by Sinn Fein. In fact Sinn Fein accused the SDLP of adopting the boycott tactic simply because they would suffer the wrath of the minority community if they had done anything different.

The SDLP response was the establishment of the New Ireland Forum with the task of redefining Irish nationalism in the light of contemporary events and attitudes. Its membership was drawn from the SDLP and the three major constitutional parties in the Republic – Fianna Fail, Fine Gael and Labour. In that respect its proponents could claim that it spoke for the vast majority of the Irish population. The Forum met for an eleven-month period in competition with the Northern Ireland Assembly and published its final report on 2 May 1984. The report did not meet universal approbation simply because it was an Irish nationalist report which expressed the age-old desire for Irish unity. In addition it suggested variants of that theme in models of federalism/confederalism and of joint Irish/British authority over Northern Ireland. The report stressed that unity could only be achieved 'in agreement' and it also provided itself with a failsafe mechanism in paragraph 5.10 when it declared its willingness 'to discuss other views which may contribute to political development'.

The New Ireland Forum helped to set the Northern Ireland political agenda by putting the onus on the British government to respond positively. In a Commons debate on 2 July 1984 John Hume stated: 'The most important aspect of the report is not the three options, but the views of Irish Nationalists about the ways in which realities must be faced if there is to be a solution.' If nothing else, the Forum exercise was a brilliant piece of public relations which commanded international attention, made much of the effort of the Assembly appear redundant, ensured that the SDLP continued to hog the limelight, and, as a corollary, halted the onward march of Sinn Fein. The latter is clear from the electoral statistics in table 1. Sinn Fein are far from being a spent force but the above suggests that where the SDLP can dictate the agenda then the republican drive loses much of its momentum. A closer examination of the figures in the context of recent events reveals that the SDLP are winning the battle inside the nationalist community. At local-government level, Sinn Fein is now the fourth largest party in the province with the capacity to run (in conjunction with the SDLP) six of the twenty-six local councils. Since local government has extremely limited powers (even by British standards) its presence may be more symbolic than real. At national level it holds only one of the seventeen Westminster seats, and undoubtedly that gives Gerry Adams a certain kudos. But its Westminster poll has been

Table 1 Sinn Fein and Social Democratic and Labour Party electoral statistics (as percentages) 1982–1987

	1982 (Assembly)	1983 (Westminster)	1984 (Europe)	1985 (Local government)	1986 (Westminster)	1987 (Westminster)
SF	10.1	13.4	13.3	11.8	6.6	9.0
SDLP	18.8	17.9	22.1	17.8	12.1	18.1

slipping in the aftermath of the Agreement, a development mirrored by its derisory 1.9 per cent of the poll when it contested the 1987 general election in the Republic.

If the SDLP's control of the agenda is one explanation for Sinn Fein's slippage, another reason lies in the activities of the IRA. A high public profile has meant that Sinn Fein spokesmen have been called upon to justify republican violence. Adams in particular calmly and articulately rationalizes and defends IRA attacks, however brutal. But this demeanour does not always square in the public mind with what is commonly understood as the democratic process. One of the most damaging reports of the New Ireland Forum exercise, for example, was entitled 'The Cost of Violence arising from the Northern Ireland Crisis since 1969'. It illustrated graphically the damage done to minority communities by the IRA in terms of fatal incidents and industrial- and commercial-sector damage done in selected towns.

It *could* be that the operation of the Agreement and the continuing debilitating effects of the Troubles may at last remove the (literally) fatal ambivalence with which a section of the nationalist community regards the Provisionals. Certainly the IRA recognizes that danger. In a Christmas message to its supporters in 1985 it described the Agreement as a 'highly sohisticated counter-revolutionary plan', designed to isolate republicans. What is self-evident is that there are no cosy relations between the SDLP and Sinn Fein, contrary to traditional practices in nationalist areas before 1969, and that bodes well for the political process.

5 Protestant Politics

Electorally, paramilitaries have not presented the same threat on the protestant side as their republican counterparts but that is not to say that the loyalist community is entirely free from the same ambivalence towards the use of violence for political ends. The powerful loyalist tradition of 'public banding', which stretches back to the seventeenth century, is based on a lack of confidence in Britain's determination to nourish the union: hence the imposition of direct rule in 1972 found a former Unionist cabinet minister, William Craig, asserting that the Ulster loyalists were 'an old and historic community' for whom union with Britain had never been 'an end in itself' but 'was always a means of preserving Ulster's British tradition and the identity of her Loyalist people'. Loyalty, therefore, took on a specific meaning so that one's primary identity was to the people and territory of Northern Ireland rather than the United Kingdom of Great Britain and Northern Ireland. One even finds a former prime minister, Lord Brookeborough, exclaiming: 'Since I've become an Ulsterman I hate the English rather more' (quoted in W. Van Voris, *Violence in Ulster: An Oral Documentary*, University of Massachusetts Press, 1975, p. 4). Such exclusiveness fails to fulfil one of the criteria for membership of the United Kingdom as laid down by a former Home Secretary, Reginald Maudling, 'that the overall authority of the Westminster parliament was recognised as in the rest of the United Kingdom' (*Memoirs*, Sidgwick and Jackson, 1978, p. 187).

Clearly, that was not the case every time Ulster loyalism faced a constitutional crisis. It was not true in 1912–14 during the Home Rule crisis; nor was it the case between 1920 and 1922 when the constitutional identity of Northern Ireland was under threat. And we shall see that as events unfolded after 1972 Ulster's loyalty was again called into question. Maudling's second criterion, that United Kingdom standards of political behaviour were accepted, was blatantly ignored time after time. To the outside world Ulster loyalism appeared strident, sectarian, aggressive and exclusivist. The paramilitary was to conduct his own brand of politics but the politician was not slow to call on the paramilitary when the times demanded. There was open collaboration during the Ulster Workers' Council (UWC) strike in May 1974 and again during the 1977 'constitutional stoppage'. Cohabitation between the paramilitaries and the politicians was resurrected in the 1980s with the creation of the 'Third Force' in 1981 (following the Anglo-Irish summit of December 1980), and of the Ulster Clubs and Ulster Resistance in the run-up to and aftermath of the signing of the Anglo-Irish Agreement. Paramilitaries had played an important role in resisting Home Rule after 1912 – although then their political masters, Sir Edward Carson and Sir James Craig, preferred to see them as an unofficial or 'provisional' army. This 'army', the Ulster Volunteer Force (UVF), moreover, had the support of many leading British Tories at that time. However, with the securing of Northern Ireland and its seeming legitimation the latterday UVF became something of an embarrassment. It re-formed in 1966 at a time of protestant working-class discontent with the prime minister's liberalizing policies and shot dead a young catholic outside a pub in the Shankill district of Belfast. Captain O'Neill promptly proscribed the organization.

The most obvious distinction between the two communities in their relationship with their 'own' paramilitaries is that loyalist paramilitaries have had a woeful record on those occasions when they have contested elections. The Vanguard Unionist Party (VUP), founded and led by the former Home Affairs Minister, William Craig, in March 1973, sat on the

Ulster Loyalist Central Co-ordinating Committee along with representatives of the paramilitary Ulster Defence Association (UDA) and many of those shop stewards who initiated the UWC strike in 1974. Vanguard won seven seats (out of seventy-eight) in the Northern Ireland Assemby elections in March 1973. That increased to fourteen in 1975 but within a year the party had declined to a rump, split on whether it should temporarily share power with the SDLP. In 1979 its last elected representative, William Craig, lost his Westminster seat. Another example is that of the Volunteer Political Party, the political wing of the UVF, formed in April 1974, shortly after the UVF had been 'deproscribed'. Its chairman, Ken Gibson, contested the October 1974 Westminster election but took only 2,690 votes, one in seven of the protestant vote. That appeared to be the end of that particular party and within a year the UVF was once again declared an illegal organization. When the UDA have contested seats they have met a similar fate, so that by the 1980s there are no more than a handful of elected representatives (from a total of 526 local councillors) with overt paramilitary connections.

Does that suggest that the protestant population is more law-abiding, more constitutionally minded, more politically committed than the catholic population? There is no overwhelming evidence to endorse this viewpoint. Its political leaders have proved well capable of what John Wilkes called 'playing the popular engines' by raising a mob and publicly fearing that they might lose control of it. The loyalist population has had a long tradition of indulging in the public procession (largely through annual Orange parades) as a political gesture. The bulk of these has passed off without incident but any history of Ulster from the mid-nineteenth century is replete with incidents of a sectarian nature. With the onset of the Troubles and growing fears for the legitimacy of the Stormont regime, loyalist leaders have indulged more and more in the politics of the street particularly if, like Ian Paisley, they did not possess a parliamentary platform. With the formation of the UDA several of these marches were headed by masked and becudgelled men full of threat and menace. While not publicly endorsed by the

political leadership very few of these demonstrations were
unequivocally condemned by them.

'Playing the popular engine', therefore, was one device
whereby the paramilitaries might be embraced. After all, it
could be claimed legitimately that groups like the UDA were
'counter-terrorist organizations' (to quote the UDA commander, Andy Tyrie) intent only on preserving the Ulster way
of life. But if it looked as if these people might get out of control
the politicians were ready to close ranks against a paramilitary
takeover. The United Ulster Unionist Council (UUUC),
formed to contest the February 1974 general election and composed of the anti-powersharing Ulster Unionist Party, the
Democratic Unionists and Vanguard, really came into its own
following the UWC victory in May. Concern that the paramilitaries might move more prominently into the political
arena and control the agenda (as well as constituency seats)
concentrated the mind wonderfully as the established politicians worked out a pact to conduct the Northern Ireland Convention election of May 1975. Having seen off the potential
paramilitary challenge the parties returned to their internecine
battles, and in May 1977 Official Unionist candidates stood in
the local government elections without UUUC endorsement.
By June it was accepted that the UUUC was dead but since the
paramilitaries no longer presented an electoral threat its
passing went largely unremarked.

A notable feature of the paramilitary role in the political
sphere has been the UDA's capacity for original and progressive thought. Twice in the past decade when political dialogue
has been sterile or nonexistent the UDA's 'think tank' has produced interesting documents. In March 1979 the New Ulster
Political Research Group (NUPRG) published a set of constitutional ideas, 'Beyond The Religious Divide'. The document
plumps for Ulster's independence as offering the best prospect
for peace and stability. It suggests a constitution based on the
US system of a separation of powers, a committee arrangement
based on proportionality and a bill of rights. Its viability might
be questioned but it was a genuine attempt to break the log jam.

More significantly, in the wake of the negative and destructive protests against the Anglo-Irish Agreement the NUPRG's successor, the Ulster Political Research Group, has produced a remarkable document, 'Common Sense' (January 1987), which argued for an agreed process of government for Northern Ireland based on co-determination, on powersharing, on a bill of rights and a mutually agreed system for the administration of justice. It accepts the reality that the whole community is part of the process, that an exclusivist mentality is counter-productive and that the Agreement could|serve as a catalyst. The impact of 'Common Sense' was such that it goaded the mainstream unionist parties into seeking positive alternatives to the Agreement. The first fruits of this process has been the publication of a Unionist Task Force document, 'An End To Drift', in July 1987. The authors, Peter Robinson and Harold McCusker, deputy leaders of the Democratic and Ulster Unionist parties respectively, and Frank Millar, chief executive of the Ulster Unionist Party, display a measure of realism and flexibility which had been missing from the unionist leadership for some considerable time.

Since the beginning of the Troubles a bitter and divisive battle has gone on for control of the unionist leadership. We must remember that the Ulster Unionist Party had been the most successful political party in liberal democracies since the 1920s. It had had absolute control of Northern Ireland until 1972. There had been the rare occasion when its dominance had been challenged by loyalist usurpers but all of them had been seen off the stage. Proportional representation for Stormont seats had been abolished before the third general election in 1929, for example, not because the party feared a nationalist revival but because it wanted to ensure that no other group could take on the mantle of defender of the constitution. In 1938 a Progressive Unionist Party contested twelve Stormont seats on a non-sectarian and radical economic programme but it failed to unseat any of the official candidates. Some working-class constituencies elected maverick candidates from time to time but virtually all of them were contained within the party straitjacket.

An exception to this rule was to be the Reverend Ian Paisley.

He represented a fundamentalist strain in Irish protestantism which has been voluble since the rise of mass democracy. Whereas others have confined their roles largely to pressure-group activity he has been the first to direct a clear and sustained challenge on the unionist citadel through his own mass party organization – the Protestant Unionist Party which contested four local-government seats in Belfast in 1964 and in a bid to broaden its electoral appeal became the Democratic Unionist Party in 1971. It was the uncertainty concerning Northern Ireland's constitutional status and the perceived threat of a republican upsurge which brought him into politics. He personified and enlarged protestant fears in a period of great political uncertainty through simplistic and negative messages. He has had the great advantage that he has never served in government. As we shall see he and his party have been beneficiaries of fortuitous circumstances and he has grasped whatever opportunities, no matter how dubious, have come along.

Since the introduction of direct rule in 1972, Northern Ireland appears to have been in a perpetual state of electioneering. There have been four local council contests (1973, 1977, 1981 and 1985) and three Stormont-type elections: for the Northern Ireland Assembly in 1973 and again in 1982, and the Northern Ireland Constitutional Convention in 1975. In addition, general elections for the Westminster parliament were fought in February and October 1974, in 1979, 1983, 1987, and a series of fifteen by-elections on 23 January 1986 called as a result of the resignations of the sitting loyalist members protesting against the imposition of the Anglo-Irish Agreement. Finally, two elections have been held for the European Parliament. Two types of electoral system have been implemented: the British plurality system for Westminster elections; and the single-transferable-vote system of proportional representation for the rest. If nothing else the electorate has gained a certain sophistication and parties have acquired vital experience in fighting elections.

One of the first advantages which the recently founded DUP enjoyed was the introduction of proportional representation.

Originally the electoral system was changed to encourage the growth of a nonsectarian middle ground. The creation of the biconfessional Alliance Party in 1970 was expected to fill this role but like other centre parties in Northern Ireland it has suffered from the fact that the middle ground is largely mythical. A secondary reason for the introduction of proportional representation was the destruction of the unionist monolith. In that it succeeded, as the results of the 1973 Assembly elections indicate. Where there had been one dominant Unionist Party up to and including 1969 (although then there had been pro- and anti-O'Neill factions) now there were no less than four unionist parties (and one independent loyalist) occupying fifty of the seventy-eight seats in the Assembly. Three of these parties, Vanguard with seven seats, DUP with eight and anti-White-Paper Unionists with eleven plus the independent candidate occupied a solid bloc of seats united in their total rejection of the government's plan to establish a powersharing administration in Northern Ireland and to recognize that there was an Irish dimension whereby the government of the Republic had some role to play in the government of the North. In opposition to this bloc were the Faulkner Unionists who were committed to negotiating with other parties within the limits laid down in the White Paper. They believed themselves to be the heirs of the Ulster Unionist Party and held only twenty-three seats, a sad reflection on the divisions within the unionist 'family' exacerbated by the introduction of proportional representation.

So, the new electoral system had one desired result in that unionists had never been more visibly divided at any stage in their history. But it was won at the cost of enabling nascent parties propounding extremist views to find their place in the sun. The irony in all of this was that initially Ian Paisley had campaigned against the introduction of proportional representation since it was 'un-British'. He was to tell his tenth Annual Party Conference some years later that it was the providence of God which secured the introduction of proportional representation. A further consequence of this division was that it left the way open for someone or some party to exploit the divisions in unionism in an attempt to claim leadership of all unionists. Ian Paisley pursued this policy ruthlessly and in doing so saw off other pretenders to the crown so that by 1987 the protestant community was fairly evenly divided between the Ulster Unionists and Democratic Unionists. The intensity of this battle led to such acrimony and exaggerated pledges that a rational debate became impossible within the camp. As a result unionists tried to outbid each other in their claims to be the true loyalists. In turn this induced unrealistic expectations of what they might secure from the government in terms of their political future *and* it made them incapable of negotiating a meaningful compromise with their political opponents. None of this was to become apparent until the meaning of the Anglo-Irish Agreement was revealed.

Following the UWC strike in 1974 unionists had some reason to believe that collectively they were capable of exercising a veto on any government decision which was not to their liking. But its very success induced a sense of complacency and of rivalry among the various factions. The politician most connected with the strike was William Craig: Ian Paisley had absented himself from the first few days of the stoppage and was not wholly trusted by the strikers. The real strength of factionalism was revealed in the 1975 elections for a Northern Ireland Constitutional Convention, established by the government in an effort to stem loyalist paramilitary euphoria and to encourage the politicians to write their own constitution for a future Northern Ireland government. In the event Vanguard took two more seats than the DUP – fourteen and twelve respectively – with a smaller percentage of the vote, and the reconstituted Official Unionists, now led by Harry West, took nineteen seats. The DUP was soon to recover the lost ground when William Craig made a fateful mistake in negotiations with the SDLP during the Convention. He suggested that there could be a powersharing government with the SDLP for the length of the emergency, in line with British political practice during the two World Wars. This was portrayed by other loyalists as a sign of appeasement, and the gesture split apart his own party. Craig never recovered.

Following the collapse of the Convention there were no further efforts made to resurrect devolved government until 1982. The battle within Unionism was now a two-horse race between the DUP and the UUP. Paisleyite tactics were based on a form of leadership destruction. One of his earliest slogans had been 'O'Neill must go'. It was to be followed at regular intervals by calls for the resignation of successive Unionist leaders – Chichester-Clark, Faulkner and West. All of them went in time but their departures could not be laid solely at the feet of Ian Paisley, much as he liked to claim the credit. The fact of the matter was that these individuals all represented an indigenous government which had allowed itself to be brought down by a combination of civil-rights cajolery and British wimpishness. They were easy targets to attack because they had to deal with the complex problems of actual government or the assumed leadership of the unionist people. If there had to be scapegoats they were the most easily identified as such. Besides the Ulster Unionist Party had undergone a genuine trauma. Out of office for the first time since 1920, rudderless and uncertain of which way to jump they seemed to lack both principle and moral fibre. Paisleyism offered certainty.

One fundamental question for *all* unionists since the imposition of direct rule was their meaning of unionism and how it should manifest itself. The debate broke down roughly into three camps – those who favoured an independent state, those who wanted devolution and those who desired integration into the British system in a manner akin to Scotland and Wales. The first option has never been too popular if only because the economics of independence was too bleak to contemplate. It remains as a fallback position to be considered only in a dire emergency. As direct rule became more permanent and the British government laid out the lines of its policy devolutionists became conscious of the fact that there would never be a return to the old Stormont system. Their internal debate has centred on the degree of power and responsibility they are prepared to concede to the minority. The 'debate', it needs to be said, has been conducted *sotto voce* and with no great enthusiasm but it has the merit of displaying a modicum of realism. The integrationists have evaded this despotism of fact since in their United Kingdom there is no need for devolved structures, and hence no need to share power. They seem oblivious to the fact that opinion polls from Britain suggest that very few indeed of the British electorate welcome closer links with Northern Ireland. Similarly MPs have not been noted for their rush to promote the integrationist case. Instead integrationists have reverted to a hazy nostalgia and have adopted Sir Edward Carson as their mentor. Devolution, they assert, was a device foistered on the province by Britain which unionists in 1920 did not seek. There is some historic merit in this argument but it ignores the fact that by the mid-1920s, when unionists saw the benefit of controlling their own destiny virtually free of Westminster's interference, they became enthusiastic devolutionists. A 1936 report of the Ulster Unionist Council sums up this attitude: 'Northern Ireland without a Parliament of her own would be a standing temptation to certain British Politicians to make another bid for a final settlement with the Irish Republic.'

In the absence of any proper surveillance from Westminster and the lack of any critical unionist opposition these questions could be set aside. All of that changed, of course, with direct rule and it was the flagship of unionism, the Ulster Unionist Party, which had to carry the brunt of the debate. This was to have relevance to the intra-unionist battle since it gave the DUP another weapon to undermine UUP morale. We have seen that the DUP had certain advantages. Since it had not been in government – nor even in existence then it could not be held responsible for the civil rights debacle. Nor had it spawned the 'traitor' O'Neill and his weak-kneed successors. Indeed one of the striking differences in the two parties was the nature and security of the leadership. The Ulster Unionist Party had from its inception been a 'bottom up' party – that is, its leaders had to keep in close touch with grassroots opinion. After all it was the Orange lodges with their fraternal instincts which had launched and sustained the party; and it was devolu- tion and a highly decentralized local-government structure which added to the sense of importance of the individual activist. The DUP, on the other hand, was very much the property of its leader, Ian Paisley. His undoubted rhetorical and organizational gifts gave him total command over the rank and file. When he spoke the party spoke.

The UUP had a second problem. It had always had very strong Westminster representation so that in the absence of devolved institutions for most of the period after 1972 its MPs saw Westminster as the real seat of power. They had some reason to do so. They enjoyed very good relations with the Conservative Party and had taken the party whip for decades. By the late 1970s the imposition of direct rule and the Ted Heath interregnum were seen as hiccups which had been overcome satisfactorily. Since the October 1974 general election Unionists probably had a much higher profile in the Commons than other regional parties because from then on they had an MP, Enoch Powell, who was an outstanding parliamentarian. In addition, they held a pivotal position of a bloc of ten votes in a parliament in which the Labour government was struggling to hold on to a majority. The unionist bloc was able to trade these seats in return for a promise that Northern Ireland's representation at Westminster would be increased to seventeen seats. Here were the palpable signs of political clout. Further, the Conservative spokesman on Northern Ireland from 1975, Airey Neave, was a convinced integrationist who had the ear of the new Tory leader, Margaret Thatcher. He had a plan to restore some of the lost powers to local government in the province and to integrate the system more fully into the British. In these circumstances integrationism became popular with the unionist leadership. Many of the secondary leadership, however, those who would aspire to a seat in a devolved institution, found no outlet for their talents beyond the small pond of local government. There was, too, a political objection to integration. It was the Commons and the government which had signed the Sunningdale agreement and which was later to be party to the Anglo-Irish Agreement. How could a small bloc of provincial MPs overturn the might of Westminster? It was precisely this worry which enabled Ian Paisley persuade his own party to engage wholeheartedly in the Northern Ireland Assembly created by James Prior. It would, he said, be 'a bulwark for the Union'; it would give the unionist family another platform with which to negotiate with the British. As a corollary, it would emphasize the distinctiveness of 'Ulster', a concept which was gaining greater popularity as more loyalists came to mistrust the British. In that sense the devolutionists could embrace those who favoured independence.

It is against this background that we examine the contest between the DUP and the UUP. The Northern Ireland Constitutional Convention was formally dissolved by Westminster Order on 9 March 1976. It was to be more than six years before another attempt at devolution was made. At that time the DUP had one paid political representative, Ian Paisley, MP for Antrim North. The party had won twenty-one out of the 526 seats at the 1973 local council elections and appeared as little more than a minor irritant on the unionist periphery. Yet by 1979 they held three Westminster seats and were the second most powerful grouping in unionist-controlled local councils with seventy-four seats and 12.7 per cent of the vote. More significantly, Ian Paisley had inflicted a very damaging blow to the UUP leadership when he topped the poll in the direct elections to the European Parliament with a massive 170,688 first preference votes, almost 30 per cent of the total. It enabled him to proclaim that he was the most popular loyalist leader ever and that his victory had been engineered by the mysterious providence of God. No longer could he be ignored or patronized by respectable unionists. He had reached the high ground and would make the running. He had been making the running before this, of course. He had led the 1977 'constitutional stoppage' with the overt support of the paramilitary UDA who wished to persuade the authorities to go on the offensive against the IRA and to restore Stormont. He undertook this adventure without the backing of the mainstream unionist parties and the rift between them led to the disbanding of the UUUC. It also contributed to deep personal animosity between Paisley and Powell, who later was to describe Paisley as 'the most resourceful, inveterate and dangerous enemy of the Union'. And yet we have seen that one month later, in the first real free-for-all contest between the unionist parties at the local council elections, the DUP did remarkably well. Steve Bruce, a relatively sympathetic academic observer of Paisleyism, explains it thus: 'because he was still *ideologically sound*, strategic and tactical mistakes could be forgiven' (*God Save Ulster! The Religion and Politics of Paisleyism*, Oxford, 1986, p. 115).

Again, in the aftermath of the Provisionals' assassination of the Reverend Robert Bradford, UUP MP for Belfast South, and of the burgeoning Anglo-Irish process, Paisley established a 'Third Force' ostensibly to complement the official security effort. Later his party was connected with Ulster Resistance, a shadowy organization opposed to the Hillsborough Agreement. None of this activity seemed to damage the electoral prospects of his party, and in the 1984 European election he increased his personal vote to 33.6 per cent. But it may be that the DUP vote had reached its plateau, as the statistics in table 2 reveal. These figures must be handled with some caution. In the first place we have not included the 1984 European election where, as we have observed, the DUP leader does exceptionally well. Secondly, 1986 was an artificial election in that the fifteen resigning MPs were contesting their old seats so that for the most part the result was inevitable. The opposition parties declined to stand in every constituency, and since the unionists wanted the contest to serve as a referendum, bogus candidates, all of them standing under the name Peter Barry (the Republic's Minister for Foreign Affairs and Co-Chairman of the Anglo-Irish Conference) were chosen to bring out the maximum vote. This did not always happen. A better comparison is between 1983 and 1987, and here the DUP are down more than 8 per cent, whereas the UUP are up almost 4 per cent. It may be argued that the DUP have lost no seats, but the following important fact needs to be borne in mind: in 1983 DUP candidates had run a number of UUP candidates a very close second and hence they looked forward to challenging them in 1987. But the two party leaders, Ian Paisley and James Molyneaux, had agreed an electoral pact that there was to be a united loyalist front against the Anglo-Irish Agreement, and so no sitting MPs were to be challenged. This proved to be a major concession to the UUP who could easily have lost two

Table 2 UUP and DUP electoral statistics (as percentages) 1982–1987

	1982 (Assembly)	1983 (Westminster)	1985 (Local goverment)	1986 (Westminster)	1987 (Westminster)
UUP	29.7	34.0	29.4	51.7	37.8
DUP	23.0	20.0	24.3	14.6	11.7

seats to the DUP and with them a further drain on party morale. In the circumstances it was the DUP morale which suffered and a number of their more promising younger members deserted the party.

This leads to one final comment. The DUP tactic of demanding the resignation of one unionist leader after another seems to have ground to a halt largely because the incumbent since 1979, James Molyneaux, has proved too wily for Ian Paisley. Molyneaux seems to be the antithesis of Paisley, colourless and lacklustre, but he has displayed considerable talent in holding his fissiparous party together at a period when it was split on tactics, on ideology and on personality. Molyneaux simply let the DUP make all the running whether at the parapolitical or extra-parliamentary level. In doing this he preserved the unity of his party, but the price that he paid may have been an inability to read the political landscape correctly and to be in a position to negotiate from strength. It is as if the unionist parties engaged in their own form of frenzied dialogue and thereby lost a sense of perspective.

This chapter and the previous one have concentrated on two discrete contests inside each community, both of them preserving their own sense of integrity and their own intensity. But the constitutional wing of the minority, the SDLP, at least raised its head above the parapet and sought assistance and solutions outside the narrow ground of provincial politics. That may explain its relative success, both in meeting head-on the ambivalence towards violence in its own community and in gaining exogenous allies. Missing from the political equation has been what are called middle-ground parties. We have noted that proportional representation was introduced to expand the mythical centre, but by 1987 it continued to remain mythical. Edward Moxon-Browne's portrait of the Alliance Party as being middle-aged, Belfast-centred, non-manual and possessing a higher proportion of the higher educated than the other parties may explain why it was not successful. It did not seem to relate to the emotions of the combatants, and it was this self-conscious thrust towards reasons and reasonableness which may have made it redundant. In that respect it was not much different from earlier 'centre' parties, like the Ulster Liberals and the Northern Ireland Labour Party (NILP). The latter held four of the fifty-two Stormont seats in the early 1960s but was swept aside in the emotion engendered by the civil rights movement. Alliance has suffered a similar fate. When inter-communal tensions rise Alliance support dips. It took 9.2 per cent of the vote in the 1973 Assembly elections and played a useful role in the powersharing executive. But while it can hope to muster about 10 per cent of the total vote this does not translate into very many seats, especially in elections conducted under the first-past-the-post system. Its best hope lies in a devolved system when it can expect to raise its visibility as it did with its ten members in the Assembly which met in 1982. It cannot, however, expect to form a government at some future date.

It may seem that we have spent too much time in the chapters on nationalist and unionist politics fishing around the extremes. The fact of the matter, as Richard Rose explained in 1976, is that Northern Ireland's party system is different from that in any other western nation: 'It more nearly resembles the party system of a Latin American country, where military and foreign involvement in politics are taken for granted, or that of Weimar Germany or the First Austrian Republic between the wars when armed groups competed with parties for the power to rule' (*Northern Ireland: A Time of Choice*, Macmillan, 1976, p. 69). Northern Ireland is not quite as stark as that, but there can be little question that the party system and its relationship to paramilitarism reflects the harsh and unstable political environment in which it operates.

6 Keeping the Peace

At its most simplistic level, and at the level of many popular British perceptions, the chief security challenge in Northern Ireland is posed by the 250 or so serving volunteers – gunmen, bombers and so on – of the Provisional IRA. It follows, therefore, that all the security forces have to do to 'solve' the Northern Ireland problem is to eliminate these volunteers. But the challenge is, in reality, much more complex. Although the Provisionals constitute the single most important terrorist organization in the province, they are as much a symptom of 'the Troubles' as a cause. We have already noted the significance of violence in Irish, and Northern Irish, political culture. The Provisionals, together with other republican and loyalist paramilitary groups, express the pragmatic and continuing faith which some political activists in the island retain in the usefulness of violent methods. In the past, violence, actual or threatened, has been effective for both republicans and loyalists and a significant number of such people evidently believe that it will continue to be so in the future. Whatever happens in the political sphere, 'hard core' paramilitaries may very well retain this romantic faith for ever and continue to present a classic 'military' or terrorist challenge to the security forces, which in turn will stimulate a straightforward police/military response. But equally important in any security effort is the need to provide effective – and therefore broadly accepted – constitutional mechanisms for the expression of legitimate political aspirations. Since the challenge in fact is both violent and political, so the response must also reflect this duality.

The three main republican paramilitary groups – the Official IRA, the Irish National Liberation Army and the Provisional IRA – illustrate the complexities of the security challenge from the nationalist side. By the late 1960s the old IRA, which after the formation of the Provisionals became known as the Official IRA, had largely abandoned its commitment to an armed struggle in favour of a Marxist political strategy promoted by the chief of staff, Cathal Goulding. Although after 1969 it embarked on a violent campaign against the army and the RUC in May 1972 the organization declared a unilateral ceasefire, asserting that continued violence was an impediment to the development of working-class solidarity. The political wing of the Officials has subsequently developed into the Workers' Party, which has representatives in the Dublin parliament. It has also conducted high-profile political campaigns in the North, although it has consistently failed to attract much electoral support. Since 1972 the Official IRA seems largely to have fallen into abeyance and it does not currently pose any direct security threat. In the 1980s, nevertheless, assertions have been made that the organization continues to be involved in armed robberies and protection rackets of various types.

The Irish National Liberation Army (INLA) was established in December 1974 by members of the Officials who opposed the Goulding-inspired ceasefire. The following year it also gained recruits from the Provisionals, such as Dominic McGlinchey, who were disenchanted by the Provisionals' spring ceasefire. The INLA developed as perhaps the most uncompromising and ruthless of the Northern Irish terrorist organizations, adopting a strict anti-British, anti-protestant and apparently Marxist military strategy. Despite the existence of a political wing, the Irish Republican Socialist Party, the INLA's emphasis has been on a purely military strategy and a policy of extreme terror, especially in border areas such as south Armagh, where they attacked a pentecostalist service at Darkley in November 1983, killing three worshippers and injuring seven. The INLA is not very large – police estimates put its maximum numbers at fewer than one hundred – and it suffered seriously from informers in the early 1980s. More recently its operations have been disrupted by a serious internal feud which broke out at the end of 1986 and led to a series of killings on both sides of the border.

Over the past eighteen years the Provisionals have become perhaps the most sophisticated and experienced terrorist group in western Europe. They began, however, as more of a vigilante force, organized to defend – as the Official IRA had evidently failed to do – the catholic community from attack by extreme protestant mobs. They were also prepared to take advantage of the fluid and unstable conditions produced by the civil rights agitation and the Stormont government's clumsy handling of it. Although British troops were at first cautiously welcomed in catholic areas when they were first deployed in 1969 (and, indeed, the army co-operated with known IRA leaders to keep the peace in west Belfast), when it emerged that London's policy was designed merely to reform the existing political system in Northern Ireland, rather than to sweep it away in anticipation of a united Ireland, the IRA moved on to the offensive against the British Army.

On the military side the Provisionals have pursued three main lines of attack. At the beginning their role as protectors of the catholic community soon developed into one of mobilizing the community into mass demonstrations, both violent and peaceful. Large-scale street disorder – in both protestant and catholic parts of Belfast and Derry – was characteristic of the early days of the Troubles. Although for the most part these riots were not 'organized' in any systematic sense, para-militaries from both sides certainly sought to capitalize on the disorder and opportunistically use it to promote their own ends. An outbreak of street violence, for example, might draw security-force personnel into a locality where they could be attacked by bombers or snipers. In a more general fashion the encouragement of disorder in the hope that the security forces might overreact might itself serve to radicalize the local community and in turn enhance the paramilitaries' role as protectors. In recent years, however, the incidence of widespread street unrest has dropped considerably. Even the annual demonstrations commemorating particularly sensitive anniversaries, such as that of internment on 9 August or Bloody Sunday on 30 January, are now generally marked only by sporadic street violence. With the development of a strong political side to their activity, indeed, the Provisionals have even felt it to be in their best interests to keep mass demonstrations peaceful. Riots themselves, after all, can damage and unsettle the very communities where the Provisionals seek to consolidate their support. During the 1981 hunger strikes, for example, quite broadly-based popular support was mobilized in peaceful public demonstrations behind the strikers by a 'National H-Block Committee', which comprised a broad spectrum of republican opinion, not just those sympathetic to the Provisionals. The development of Provisional Sinn Fein's political strength and the election of Provisional sympathizers to local councils would not have been so successful if the H-block demonstrations had all been violent. There remains, therefore, a certain conflict within the Provisionals' strategy between continued violence, which some believe might be most effective in persuading the British to 'get out', and more political and constitutional means through which Sinn Fein might be able to secure the mass electoral support which has so far eluded them. In other words, there is a tension between the Armalite *and* the ballot box, and the Armalite *versus* the ballot box.

The second main strand in the Provisionals' campaign of violence consists principally of bomb attacks on government, security and economic targets with the intention of so destabilizing the community that law and order, as enforced by the existing (British) authorities, completely breaks down, the British government gives up the struggle and a demoralized loyalist community acquiesces in the establishment of a united Ireland. These aims, together with the more immediate tactical advantages, were clearly set out by Sean MacStiofain in his memoirs, *Revolutionary in Ireland* (Saxon House, 1974), when he discussed the use of the car bomb – one of the principal weapons in the Provisionals' armoury. The car bomb, he recorded, was introduced in 1972 both for strategic and tactical reasons.

The strategic aim was to make the government and adminstration of the occupied North as difficult as possible, simultaneously striking at its colonial economic structure. The British government was ultimately responsible for all compensation for bomb damage. The tactical reason was that the introduction of the car bomb tied down large numbers of British troops in the centre of Belfast and other large towns. While they were stuck there on guard duties, fewer soldiers would be available for offensive counter-insurgency operations or for harassing the people in nationalist areas under the psychological saturation policy. (p. 243)

1972 has been the worst year during the present troubles. There were nearly 1,400 explosions and the security forces neutralized another 500 bombs. Two attacks by the Provisionals during July demonstrate both the vulnerability of the community to car bombs and the human costs of such attacks. On 'Bloody Friday', 21 July, nineteen bombs went off in Belfast, largely without warning. Seven civilians and two soldiers were killed, while 130 people were injured. On 31 July, three car bombs exploded without warning in the village of Claudy, county Derry. Seven civilians died and twenty-nine were injured. The Provisionals have tried to explain incidents such as these by blaming British 'black' propaganda and alleged security-force delays in passing on bomb warnings, but they also admit that innocent civilians may suffer in the 'war against British imperialism'. Undoubtedly, however, attacks where there are heavy civilian casualties tend to alienate the Provisionals even from the republican community and in recent years the damage caused by car bombs – the incidence of which has in any case dropped – has mostly been confined to property. Improved security procedures have also reduced the impact of such attacks. Unattended parking is prohibited in most town centres and the area around public buildings is generally specially protected, although this can never be a guarantee against attack. Shortly before Christmas in 1986 a bomb on a hijacked school bus destroyed Lisburn Road police station in Belfast and damaged several hundred houses.

For the terrorists, the employment of car bombs reflects the weaponry available to them. Much of the explosive used in Northern Ireland is home-made, based on agricultural fertilizers, with comparatively low explosive power. Bombs are often very heavy – a 1,000-lb bomb is not uncommon – and can only be delivered to the target by vehicle. The very bulk of the explosives makes it correspondingly difficult for the terrorists to store supplies. In July 1987 police discovered a ton of explosives stored in an underground steel-lined chamber on the Republic side of the border. When supplies of explosive are particularly restricted, as in 1977–8, the Provisionals may opt for fire bombs such as the blast incendiary which caused considerable damage to commercial premises in their 1977 Christmas campaign. This device consisted of a small explosive charge attached to a can of petrol which could send a ball of fire bursting into the target. In February 1978 a device such as this was detonated at the La Mon House restaurant near Comber, county Down. Twelve people were burnt to death and twenty-three seriously injured. Public reaction was so strong that the Provisionals were obliged to call off their fire-bomb campaign. Bombs, especially large ones, despite the difficulties in planting them and their frequently unpredictable results, will remain an important weapon for the Provisionals since they provide the best means of scoring 'spectaculars': morale-boosting successes which attract the widest international publicity, such as the attack on Mrs Thatcher at the Grand Hotel, Brighton, during the 1984 Conservative Party conference.

The third strand in the Provisionals' strategy is to attack those whom they see as the servants of British imperialism. This definition is very broadly drawn, extending as it does from full-time members of the army and police to judges and magistrates, prison officers and civilian employees of the security forces. During the summer of 1986, moreover, a particular campaign was waged against contractors working on government buildings and even shopkeepers and traders supplying goods to the army and police. Clearly attacks on senior political, diplomatic and legal figures have great attractions for the Provisionals. The Brighton bomb, the killings of the British ambassador, Christopher Ewart-Biggs, in Dublin in July 1976 and Lord Mountbatten on August Bank Holiday 1979, and that of the second most senior Northern Ireland judge, Lord Justice Gibson, in April 1987 are held by Provisionals to be among their greatest successes as they have struck at the heart of the British establishment and such attacks will certainly remain an important part of the Provisionals' campaign in the future. Bombings in England generally serve a similar purpose, although the killing of civilians, such as in the Harrods bomb in December 1983, invariably provokes a hostile public reaction.

The most regular targets for Provisional violence, however, are members of the security forces. Over the whole period of the Troubles, up to the end of August 1987, 804 members of the security forces have died. Of these nearly half (389) were members of the regular army, while the rest came from the RUC (249) and the UDR (166). But the pattern of these casualties has changed markedly over the years. In the first place the total number of security-force deaths and injuries has dropped substantially from the peak year of 1972 when 146 security personnel (and 321 civilians) died and nearly 5,000 people of all sorts were injured. Since 1980 the number of people killed in any one year has never exceeded one hundred and the *average* annual number of deaths (for 1980–6) has been seventy-five. Within the security-force casualties there has been a major shift away from regular-army personnel to locally recruited people – police and members of the UDR. Over the seven years 1980–6, fifty-nine regular army soldiers have died (an average of about eight per year), sixty-one members of the UDR (nine per year) and 103 policemen and women (fifteen per year). Apart from improved security procedures – the Provisionals would clearly kill more such people if they could – this change reflects the increasing 'Ulsterization' of the security effort.

Ulsterization grew out of an official reassessment of the security effort in the mid-1970s, which mirrored a similar process within the Provisional movement. The Provisionals' strategy of the early 1970s, which aimed at a complete breakdown of government, depended on a large body of active IRA volunteers particularly in order to mobilize mass community demonstrations. This organization proved to be highly insecure and easily penetrated by the security and intelligence agencies. In 1976–7 there was a review of strategy after which the Provisionals adopted their current 'long haul' approach in which a continued war of attrition against the security forces and related targets has been combined with the development of an overt political organization. The terrorist side of this strategy led to the adoption of a smaller and more secure cellular organization, composed of compact 'active service units'.

On the government side a working party was set up in 1976 to examine the future direction of strategy. The resulting policy contained two main strands which have remained important ever since: Ulsterization and criminalization. The abolition of internment and the 'special category status' enjoyed by paramilitary prisoners since mid-1972 eroded the officially-recognized distinction between 'political' and 'ordinary' crime. Nevertheless, the legal process itself effectively distinguishes between these types of crime. Since 1973 terrorist (or 'scheduled') offences have been dealt with in special non-jury courts, popularly known as 'Diplock' courts. Following the imposition of direct rule in 1972, the government appointed a British judge, Lord Diplock, to head an inquiry into legal aspects of the government's response to political violence. Concerned with the intimidation of witnesses and jurors, Diplock proposed the temporary establishment of non-jury courts for the duration of the Troubles. These courts still operate today. In the first instance people are tried before a judge sitting alone, while all appeals are heard before three judges. This contrasts with the situation in the Republic's non-jury courts for terrorist offences where three judges sit throughout.

The policy of Ulsterization indicated London's desire for local security forces to take on an increasing share of operations in Northern Ireland and this is reflected in the changed numerical weight of the various security forces. The number of regular army troops reached a maximum of 21,800 in July 1972. During the late 1970s there was a gradual decline and the current (mid-1987) number of soldiers stands at approximately 10,000. The size of the UDR has also declined over the same period, although less dramatically. In 1972 the regiment had nearly 9,000 members. Today, it has 6,500. But police numbers have increased, from approximately 3,000 at the beginning of the troubles to over 12,000 today. The great majority of security-force personnel are now locally raised and, indeed, live within the community itself. When off duty they represent attractive 'soft' targets for the terrorists. In the immediate aftermath of the Anglo-Irish Agreement, too, RUC personnel living in protestant neighbourhoods (as most do) became targets of attack from loyalists bitterly opposed to the Agreement.

The denominational composition of the local security forces has a clear impact on their effectiveness as communal peacekeepers. The UDR, which is almost entirely protestant, has frequently been characterized by nationalists as little more than a re-formed 'B' Specials, composed of ill-disciplined loyalist extremists. Certainly many former members of the Specials joined the UDR when it was first set up in 1970 and a worryingly large number of UDR personnel have been implicated in loyalist violence. Eleven UDR men, for example, have been convicted of murder. During its sixteen-year life there has been a very considerable turnover of personnel in the UDR with comfortably over 30,000 men and women having served in it. The army's official view is that while some unsatisfactory people have undoubtedly passed through the regiment, the current controls on recruitment and internal discipline ensure that the unit performs its duties as impartially as possible. The UDR, in any case, is not used in all types of security duties. It is not employed for riot control and is mainly deployed in routine patrolling, manning vehicle checkpoints and guarding static installations.

Although by no means accepted as fully impartial throughout the catholic community, the RUC is regarded as a much more acceptable force than the UDR. An opinion poll taken for the *Belfast Telegraph* in early 1985 reported that 47 per cent of catholics believed that the police were performing their duties fairly. The proportion of catholics in the force has never been very high. In 1969 the number was 11 per cent, and it is estimated that the current level is substantially the same, although there is a rather higher proportion in the higher ranks. Clearly any satisfactory resolution of the security problem depends on the police being fully established as an acceptable service throughout Northern Ireland. The increasing professionalization and modernization of the force following the disasters of the late 1960s has gone a considerable way towards establishing the RUC as an impartial and widely-respected body.

With Ulsterization the chief responsibility for security has steadily been transferred to the RUC under a policy known as 'the primacy of the police'. Since 1977 the day-to-day direction of policy has been in the hands of a security co-ordinating committee, chaired by the Chief Constable, who, in consultation with the GOC, reports to the Secretary of State. The new strategy has not been entirely trouble-free. There has been friction between army and police, and differences over the general thrust of security policy. In the summer of 1979, for example, the GOC, Sir Timothy Creasey, was arguing that 'police primacy' actually impeded an efficient security effort and that a more 'military' policy would, in the long run, prove to be more effective. The appointment of the old intelligence hand, Sir Maurice Oldfield (head of the Secret Intelligence Service, 1973–7), to be 'security co-ordinator' in October 1979 was partly in order to reduce police–army tension, but it also stemmed from the government's review of security following the assassination of Lord Mountbatten and the bomb attack at Warrenpoint which killed eighteen soldiers on 27 August 1979. Oldfield's appointment, and the arrival of new men – Sir Richard Lawson and Jack (now Sir John) Hermon – to head the army and police restored a co-operative atmosphere to the security forces. It is perhaps the case that, as an intelligence veteran, Oldfield was better qualified than a policeman or a soldier to appreciate the need for the closest possible co-ordination of the security effort. He retired in the summer of 1980 when he was succeeded by Sir Brooks Richards, who had previously been intelligence co-ordinator in the cabinet office. The post lapsed in 1981, by which time co-ordination between the different security elements had greatly improved.

With the shift in unrest away from street violence towards the more focused PIRA attacks on carefully-selected targets, the army has lost most of its riot-control responsibilities and has become extensively committed to covert surveillance and operational duties. The Special Air Service Regiment (SAS) has, as might be expected, provided specialist assistance in this area. Individual SAS officers helped train army-intelligence units in the early 1970s and in 1969 a squad of the regiment served in the province for a few weeks. But the regiment was not formally deployed in Northern Ireland until 1976 when, in response to an upsurge of violence in South Armagh, the prime minster, Harold Wilson, announced that SAS troops were to be employed in 'patrolling and surveillance' tasks. The SAS by their training are especially well suited for long-term covert surveillance operations, and they have served continuously in the province since 1976. It is difficult to assess the impact of these troops in Northern Ireland since information about SAS activities is mostly classified. Military opinion asserts that they have markedly assisted the security effort 'both in gathering vital information and in direct offensive operations against the IRA'. It also appears that the psychological effect of their deployment has been out of all proportion to the actual numbers of personnel involved. The popular mass media, indeed, are inclined to describe all covert army operations as 'SAS' actions, while in fact the SAS's role has largely been confined to providing training of troops from other regiments who are then deployed on what might be described as 'SAS-type' duties.

The enhanced emphasis on the covert and intelligence side of security operations has placed a particular premium on informers. In Northern Ireland in the 1980s they assumed a particular significance in the so-called 'supergrass' or converted-terrorist system. In this case the government had informers who were evidently providing a great deal of high-grade intelligence. The problem was how best this should be used. In keeping with the policy of attempting to convict as many terrorists as possible, the authorities used the information as criminal intelligence to charge and try a substantial number of terrorist suspects. Between November 1981 and

November 1983 nearly 600 people were arrested on information supplied by seven loyalist and eighteen republican supergrasses. Fifteen of these informers, however, retracted their evidence and a significant number of convictions secured on uncorroborated evidence were overturned on appeal. The overall conviction rate for the ten supergrass trials, taking appeals into account, was 44 per cent, not sufficiently high to warrant the very considerable investment of resources in the process. One informer, for example, Joseph Bennett (a former loyalist paramilitary who had been granted immunity for his own offences), was given a new name and corroborating documents by the RUC Special Branch, who also bought him a house in England and paid him a stipend. In 1986 there were reports that £30,000 had been paid to a single informer. Informers undoubtedly pose problems for the terrorist organizations, which deal ruthlessly with suspected police agents. Apart from numerous non-fatal 'punishment shootings' (frequently in the knees), it has been calculated that the Provisionals and the INLA have 'executed' some thirty suspected informers since 1973.

In circumstances where security forces may be acquiring fairly good operational intelligence, but not of sufficient quality to use for criminal prosecutions, the authorities may be tempted to use the information either to detain suspected terrorists without trial – internment – or to inform 'special operations' against the terrorists. When internment without trial was implemented in August 1971, comparatively little was known about the recently-formed Provisionals and the information used in the initial 'sweep' was seriously out-of-date. The majority of those actually arrested (340 people) were 'old-style' republicans known for their involvement in the political side of the movement and members of the Official IRA. The Provisionals were hardly touched and the whole process was both a political and security disaster. It caused great resentment in the nationalist community and stimulated an upsurge in violence. Those actually picked up were radicalized by the experience and the internment camps themselves became 'universities of terrorism'.

From time to time allegations have been made that a 'shoot-to-kill' policy has been adopted in Northern Ireland. A particular illustration of this emerged through the report prepared by Mr John Stalker (Deputy Chief Constable of the Manchester Police) on the killing of six people by the security forces in November and December 1982. Five of the victims were known members of the IRA or the INLA. The sixth was an innocent 17-year-old youth, Michael Tighe. The security-force personnel responsible for the killings were attached to an RUC 'Headquarters Mobile Support Unit' (HQMSU), variously described in the press as a 'quick reaction squad', a 'SAS-trained undercover squad' and 'essentially a potential death squad'. In conjunction with a police section called 'E4A' (a covert deep surveillance unit), the HQMSUs were apparently under the general control of the Special Branch and worked closely with MI5 and army intelligence. The Tighe killing, for example, occurred in a barn where arms were known to have been hidden and in which MI5 technicians had planted listening devices. At the time of Tighe's death RUC and army intelligence officers were jointly monitoring these devices. The activities revealed by the Stalker inquiry demonstrate very close co-operation now between the various intelligence agencies. But they also raise questions about the command and accountability of 'special forces' which without close supervision can tend to run out of control and become a law unto themselves.

The kind of security tactics which Stalker investigated are illustrative of the increasing sophistication of the security effort. It is not just the Provisionals who have a 'long haul' strategy. The mobilization of considerable resources – both human and technical – towards carefully gathering information about the terrorist challenge has become a crucial component in security policy. Long-term covert surveillance, the recruitment of informers and the systematic collation of information from a very wide range of sources can enable the security forces to strike at the Provisionals and other illegal paramilitary organizations. One such notable success was achieved in May 1987 when a strong force of army and police ambushed an attack on Loughgall police station (county Armagh). Eight IRA men – the entire unit – and a passing motorist were killed. These were the Provisionals' worst losses in a single incident during the troubles. The security forces – like the Provisionals for their part – cannot depend on scoring many such spectacular successes. For both sides the conflict is mainly a war of attrition and no single 'military' victory will bring it to a tidy finish.

The government's continued desire that terrorists may be brought to justice through the courts indicates their appreciation of this fact. There are very considerable difficulties in marshalling enough strong evidence to secure convictions, yet in a situation where the government aims to restore the 'rule of law', there is no real alternative to working through legal channels. But the Diplock courts have come in for a very great deal of criticism from both the republican and loyalist sides, especially when the supergrass system was in operation. The issue is not so much one of the courts convicting innocent persons – there is very little evidence of this – but of the methods by which they work. It is essential, as in any free society, that justice should not only be done, but that it should be seen to be done. The streamlining of Northern Ireland's legal system to meet the difficulties presented by political violence has given rise to accusations of 'conveyor-belt justice', where the courts exist less to administer justice than to defeat terrorism. No legal system can work satisfactorily without public confidence, a point specifically recognized in the Anglo-Irish Agreement (Article 8), and the Diplock system does not now command full confidence throughout the whole community. One current proposal is that three judges should sit in the courts, but the government and the Northern Ireland judiciary have so far resisted this. Nevertheless, the administration of justice will for the foreseeable future continue to be an important item on the agenda of Anglo-Irish meetings, since it is a central component in the security effort.

The problem of public confidence applies with equal force to the RUC. Again this was recognized in the Anglo-Irish Agreement, which noted that 'there is a need for a programme of special measures in Northern Ireland to improve relations between the security forces and the community, with the object in particular of making the security forces more readily accepted by the nationalist community'. In the end the 'security forces' must primarily mean the police, since military force is inappropriate for the maintenance of law and order. Although units of the British army will continue to be stationed in Northern Ireland – as was the case before 1969 – troops ideally should only be deployed to reinforce the police in an emergency, which is the position in the rest of the United Kingdom. Northern Ireland has not yet returned to this desirable state of affairs, and may not do so for some time, but the withdrawal of troops from the streets of west Belfast, Derry and the south Armagh countryside, and their replacement (however gradually) by ordinary police, should continue to be a government priority.

7 The International Dimension

The world-wide welcome for the Anglo-Irish Agreement provides manifest evidence of an international dimension to a domestic dispute in one of the world's more stable regions. It reinforced the impression created by the selling of the Agreement itself, that if there was no great enthusiasm for it in the province where the problem existed, there was no shortage of good will among well-disposed powers and even the United Nations where the Secretary-General, Perez de Cuellar, ceremonially and simultaneously received copies from the respective British and Irish ambassadors in his headquarters within hours of the signing. On 20 December 1985 the Agreement was registered with the United Nations under Article 102 of the Charter. In the light of its dismissal by the majority of Northern Ireland's population much of this might be put down to clever public relations on the part of the various officials. Nevertheless, the presentation of the Agreement was organized by the two signatories acting in concert – an unusual enough phenomenon in the bitter and interminable saga of Anglo-Irish relations. Here, too, was proof that the Northern Ireland problem was being examined beyond 'the dreary steeples of Fermanagh and Tyrone' (to quote Winston Churchill) and with the encouragement especially of the United Kingdom. This was a remarkable advance in British attitudes since the outbreak of the Troubles. In August 1969 a joint communiqué signed by the prime ministers of the United Kingdom and of Northern Ireland affirmed that 'responsibility for affairs in Northern Ireland is entirely a matter of domestic consideration'. That was intended as a rebuff to the government of the Irish Republic which was indulging in antipartitionist rhetoric. At the United Nations, for example, the Irish foreign minister, Patrick Hillery, requested by virtue of Article 35 of the Charter 'an urgent meeting of the Security Council in connection with the situation in the *Six Counties* of Northern Ireland'. The request was rejected but the language was both emotional and deliberate: 'six counties' was meant as a diminutive in contrast with the sovereign state of the Republic of Ireland.

If the Anglo-Irish Agreement signed at Hillsborough signalled a British concessionary mentality it must be said that the Irish Republic likewise appeared more penitent. Both the Preamble and Article 1 of the Agreement recognized the majority's right to resist Irish unity. In that respect both governments had moved a long way from the mutually hectoring and contemptuous tones of the early days of the Troubles and had adopted the 'quiet diplomacy and personal conversation' approach suggested by the then Taoiseach, Jack Lynch, when he addressed the United Nations on 22 October 1970. Arriving at that state of mind did not come easily to either side given their very long history of animosity and the vast asymmetry in relationships and political and economic development between them. But by 1980 both governments put their signatures to a communique which spoke of 'the totality of relationships within these islands'. That phrase was sufficiently vague to blur the distinction between the intergovernmental and the internal, the exogenous and endogenous.

It was also sufficiently ominous to the unionist population, and it was for that reason that Ian Paisley created his Third Force and embarked on what he called the 'Carson Trail' in self-conscious emulation of Carson's leadership in the aftermath of the Third Home Rule Bill in 1912 when the Ulster Unionists actively prepared to oppose the Westminster government with armed force. But the similarity between Paisley and Carson is only superficial. The latter had the foresight or good fortune to bring a segment of the British establishment with him; Paisley's tactics were to alienate putative support in Great Britain. Whether or not that support was forthcoming does not take away from the perennial unionist doubts about the status of the territory and regime to which they gave primary loyalty.

Following the creation of Northern Ireland in 1921 unionists engaged in enhancing their status and security. They mistrusted the original Council of Ireland suggestions (whereby the governments of Belfast and Dublin were to meet on a regular basis to deal with matters of common concern) in the Government of Ireland Act of 1920 because it held out the prospect of Irish unity. But the first prime minister, Sir James Craig (later Lord Craigavon) handled the matter with some skill when he suggested that 'in all matters under the purview of the Council' each government consult each other 'on terms of equality'. The Dublin government resisted this since it feared that it would ensure a loyalist veto, and the Council of Ireland came to naught. Instead, 'independent' Ireland refused formal recognition of the Northern entity and the new Constitution formulated by the Taoiseach, Eamon de Valera, in 1937 claimed *de jure* jurisdiction over the North. That may have been to the satisfaction of the unionist leaders because it gave them a peculiar status based on fear and grievance. In any case the unionist government had been consolidating its position within the United Kingdom. Sir James Craig had assiduously played on British disdain of all things Irish and its reluctance to get involved militarily in the Irish tangle. The result was that a relationship of mutual accommodation prevailed between the sovereign government in London and the subordinate unit in Belfast. The latter acquired a large degree of security autonomy and was more or less left to its own devices. This was to have important consequences after 1969 when the British government turned its attention to conditions in Northern Ireland. Unionist politicians resented this interference because they misunderstood the nature of the Union. As a former prime minister, Brian Faulkner, described it, the illusions of the devolved system 'created unspoken separatist tendencies. It also meant that the crisis of 1969 hit an unprepared Westminster right between the eyes' (*Memoirs of a Statesman*, Weidenfeld and Nicolson, 1978, p. 26).

All of this has relevance to the situation which arose after 1969 and especially after 1972. One of the major opinion-formers, Enoch Powell, was convinced that every British act and attitude since 1972 – with the exception of granting Northern Ireland extra seats at Westminster in 1977 – 'has been designed to promote and facilitate the reintroduction of devolution in a form which could be moved or pressured into a direct relationship with the Republic . . . sweetened by a British Isles totality or a Commonwealth or an EEC or a NATO dimension' because Britain is convinced that 'the island of Ireland is vital to the "defence of the West" '. Powell unveiled this plot in the *Spectator* (8 January 1983) where he delineated the principles that guide Britain, Ireland and the USA to tease out a solution based on Irish unity. He asserts that the strategy is based on four principles: (i) the Republic cannot take Northern Ireland by force; (ii) to end partition there needs to be an autonomous Ulster with 'guarantees' in a federal Ireland, possibly in some loose relationship with Britain; (iii) United Kingdom pressure is necessary to accomplish this; but (iv) that will be exerted only when Irish unity is 'strategically necessary to Britain. The key lies in the 'defence of the West'. In numerous speeches he strove to reveal the United States' unwelcome interference in Northern Ireland's affairs. It is not our purpose to judge the validity of these claims, and in any case conspiracy theories are not easy to prove. But there can be little doubt that the international plane has taken on an added dimension as the Troubles have proceeded.

A favourite ploy of Irish diplomats in the earlier years of partition was 'to raise the sore thumb' – that is, to complain about the malign effects of partition on Ireland's development at every opportune moment during international gatherings. This procedure was based on the false premise that if Irish statesmen publicised the wrongs their country had suffered, the world would come to their assistance. That strain in Irish foreign policy has a reasonable lineage stretching back to an American tour by Eamon de Valera in 1919. Surprisingly, when the Troubles did break out the Irish used the ploy less than some might have anticipated. With the exception of the famous piece of shadow boxing between the foreign affairs minister, Patrick Hillery, and the British ambassador to the United Nations, Lord Caradon, at the UN in August 1969, and the hiring of an international public relations firm for a short period, Ireland did not indulge in this tactic. It preferred to deal directly with the British government.

One possible reason was that it was embarrassed by its own unpreparedness for the North's political violence. This was at least something it shared with London. Its level of knowledge and expertise concerning the North was abysmal – a factor which might be explained by the anomalous relationship which existed between Dublin and London for many years. Although Ireland had left the Commonwealth in 1949, as late as 1968 it was located in the British *Diplomatic Service List* under 'List of British Representatives in the Commonwealth, and the Republic of Ireland'. It seemed to enjoy a unique status, neither part of the British Commonwealth of Nations nor wholly 'foreign'. Had it been the latter then the Foreign Office would have been expected to have provided the 'amassed and living knowledge of overseas countries' which is its special contribution to the national effort. There simply was no amassed and living knowledge regarding Ireland. Until 1965, when the Foreign and Commonwealth Services were amalgamated, the British Embassy in Dublin was staffed by the Commonwealth Service and reported (until October 1968) to the Commonwealth Office. According to Sir John Peck, who was appointed ambassador in April 1970, this had a disastrous effect since during

> the first fifteen months of responsibility for relations with the Republic of Ireland, the staff of the Foreign Office had discovered that they knew very little about it. The reason was that the traditions and requirements of the Foreign Office and the Commonwealth Office had been different. The Foreign Office dealt with a world that is truly foreign – independent nations which might be stronger or weaker than Britain, friendly or hostile, but which were in any case wholly detached. The Commonwealth Office dealt with former British colonies ...

> where, as befits a member of the family, a good deal could be
> taken for granted.
>
> (*Dublin from Downing Street*, Gill and Macmillan, 1978, p. 17)

But nothing could be taken for granted in Anglo-Irish
relations.

The anomaly had arisen with Eire's decision to leave the
Commonwealth. Cabinet papers for 1948 reveal the British
government's uncertainty as to how to handle the position.
Initially it was decided that the Republic of Ireland (as it
became known) would be treated like any other foreign state.
But, after conferring with some of the Commonwealth leaders,
the decision was reversed. Apart from anything else, there were
practical difficulties for the Home Office which would have
faced formidable administrative problems if all Irish citizens
had to be treated as aliens. There were also fears that the
Republic would be in a strong position to put pressure on the
UK at the United Nations if it raised the question of partition
at the General Assembly, where it would be assured of considerable support. Britain, too, would be embarrassed if it had
to give positive support to the continuance of partition. So, for
practical, strategic and expedient reasons it would be better if it
were assumed that Ireland were still 'family'. Ireland appeared
to go along with this diplomatic fiction which was mutually
advantageous as long as the North did not explode. Once it did
all bets were off.

This explains that lack of preparedness, a problem which
was compounded as the volume of work on Ireland increased
substantially. An administrative decision that a newly created
Republic of Ireland department within the Foreign Office
should report to an under-secretary whose principal concern
was Defence and Foreign Office liaison with the Service
departments had inevitable consequences because, to quote
Peck, it 'introduced the danger that departmental advice reaching the Foreign Secretary about policy towards the Republic
would be related primarily to our military policy and interests
in the domestic law and order situation in the North' (*Dublin
from Downing Street*, p. 116). Here we have the full complexity of

the Northern Ireland problem unfolding. For unionists it was entirely an internal affair to be sorted out by a strict security policy or perhaps by tinkering with reforms. But the Foreign Office was becoming conscious of its external dimension and of its potential for embarrassment abroad.

None of this was of any great moment in 1969, and indeed it might be argued that not until 1976 or 1977 that playing the American card became significant. The reason, paradoxically, concerned the failure of political movement in Northern Ireland itself. The nature with which the powersharing government was brought down and the lack of generosity in the convention report convinced the SDLP that it would have to seek its salvation elsewhere. At its annual conference in 1977 the party adopted a more green policy when it emphasized the Irish dimension and called on the British government to spell out its long-term intentions for Northern Ireland. John Hume, then deputy leader, shifted strategy on to the international plane in an attempt to concentrate the official mind. His party adopted a threefold strategy: (i) to discourage Irish-Americans from contributing to Provisional IRA funds, (ii) to link substantial US aid to economic development in Northern Ireland if an acceptable political solution could be found and (iii) to involve the presidency in seeking out an Irish policy.

All of this seemed to come into play on 30 August 1977 when US president Jimmy Carter made a seven-paragraph statement which condemned violence and made a promise of economic aid in the event of a political solution being found. While the statement did say that there 'are no solutions that outsiders can impose' it has been recognized as going beyond America's benign neutrality in this matter and it displays an element of impatience with the lack of political movement in the province. Its publication denoted both that the Irish lobby in Washington was becoming influential and also that British interests in the United States conceded as much.

One of the features of Irish America has been its disintegrative tendency. Unlike other ethnic lobbies there has been no co-ordinated effort from the Irish simply because there is the same fundamental split as at home between constitutional and physical-force nationalists. The Irish Northern Aid Committee, more popularly known as Noraid, has been in existence since April 1970 as a fundraiser and money supplier to the IRA, although it has claimed that its resources go to the families of imprisoned IRA personnel. One knowledgeable commentator, Jack Holland (author of *The American Connection: United States Guns, Money and Influence in Northern Ireland* (Viking Penguin, 1987)), has estimated that at one time it had seventy units throughout the United States and 2,000 members in New York alone. It may have raised as much as $5 million since 1971 for the cause, so there can be little doubt that it has been of considerable benefit to the Provisional effort. Noraid shares the militant platform with a number of other groups some of which may not condone IRA violence but all of which believe that the answer to the problem of Northern Ireland is British withdrawal. These include the Ad Hoc Committee on Irish Affairs set up by Congressman Mario Biaggi in September 1977 to press for congressional hearings on the problem. Biaggi can muster as many as 120 congressional signatures on motions critical of British government policy although the number of active members of his Ad Hoc group is probably not more than ten. At the very least he can act as an extreme irritant and he is suspected by the Irish government of being a closet supporter of violence. A third group worthy of mention is the Irish National Caucus led by Father Sean McManus. It is a professional lobbying organization with offices on Capitol Hill in Washington and an impressive self-publicist in its director. Father McManus has stressed that the Northern Ireland problem is an American issue and in that respect no Irish government nor Irish politican can dictate to Irish-Americans how they should conduct their campaign. It follows that there is not much love lost between the Caucus and successive Irish governments. Indeed, even across the militant platform there are differences of personality and of strategy so that in combination they are not as powerful as their potential would suggest.

That may be one reason why the constitutionalists gathered together in the Friends of Ireland group. It is much smaller than the Ad Hoc committee but much more influential. The

Friends evolved out of what was known as the 'Four Horsemen' that is, Senators Ted Kennedy and Patrick Moynihan, House Speaker 'Tip' O'Neill and former governor of New York Hugh Carey. These four wielded huge influence in their own right so that any joint statement from them had to be taken with the utmost seriousness. At the start of the Troubles some of their remarks were highly emotional and based on lack of information. But with the support of the Irish Embassy in Washington and certain politicians, notably John Hume, they began to move beyond the simple 'Brits Out' kneejerk reaction to something more considered and constructive. Their annual St Patrick's Day statement became something of a ritual and a barometer of Irish constitutionalism's standing in America. Significantly, they devoted considerable effort in unambivalent condemnation of IRA and other violence so that the attitude of the British Embassy and governments became much more positive towards them. In that respect the British looked forward to these statements as one possible means to diminish republican support in Ireland. Unobtrusively, therefore, that which had been purely a matter of domestic consideration was now being seen as one in which Irish America had a role to play.

One problem which the constitutionalists had to face was that their support came solely from the Democrats. The day might arise when the Republican Party controlled Congress and the Presidency and Kennedy and company would have a much diminished role. Hence the move to establish the Friends with much more widespread support. It was formally launched in 1981 when republican, Ronald Reagan, was in the White House. But the President had to work closely with the House Speaker, Tip O'Neill. Their coincidence of Irish background enabled them to work in some harmony on this particular issue. In the meantime the Friends had recruited twenty members from the Senate and twenty-one from the House of Representatives.

If President Carter's August 1977 statement can be seen as establishing that the problem of Northern Ireland was a legitimate subject for concern in American foreign policy the implications did not manifest themselves for a few years. In

April 1979 in the run-up to the British general election Tip O'Neill on a visit to Ireland made some very pointed remarks about the lack of political movement in Northern Ireland and the propensity of Westminster politicians to treat it like a political football. These remarks were considered to be gross interference in the British jurisdiction and the Speaker had to endure the wrath of the Fleet Street tabloid leader writers. Nevertheless his remarks were taken seriously by the incoming prime minister, Margaret Thatcher. In her first major interview for a foreign newspaper (*New York Times*, 12 November 1979) the prime minister made no secret of her impatience: 'We will listen for a while. We hope we will get agreement. But then the Government will have to make some decisions and say "having listened to everyone, we are going ahead to try this or that" whichever we get most support for'. They went ahead with what became known as the Atkins initiative, an effort by the new secretary of state to devise another devolved Assembly with the assistance of the indigenous politicians. This sounded suspiciously like what Speaker O'Neill had demanded in April 1979 – 'an early, realistic and major initiative on the part of the incoming British government so as to get negotiations moving quickly'. That Atkins did not succeed was not altogether surprising and lack of success may even have given a stimulus to the Anglo-Irish process which got under way with two summits, May and December, in 1980.

It is the strongly held belief of some unionists that this process is part of a wider strategy. Enoch Powell, for example, has described the Foreign Office as 'the inveterate enemy of the Union' and the summit talks as part of a plan to abolish Northern Ireland and incorporate the unified country inside NATO. The beneficiary would be the United States since it would block 'the gravest of all the gaps in the American strategy for Europe'. This conspiracy theory was put at greater length by the Ulster Unionist leader, Jim Molyneaux, in a Northern Ireland Assembly debate on 22 March 1983 when he revealed that a 'high powered conference took place in London between the British and American Governments' some weeks after the Conservatives came back into power in 1979 in which

Northern Irish affairs were discussed between Lord Carrington and secretary of state, Cyrus Vance (contrary to the
declarations of successive British governments) to the effect
that the internal affairs of the United Kingdom were a matter
for the UK government and Parliament. Mr Molyneaux's
suspicions may well have been fuelled by the rapidity with
which British policy had changed. As late as 5 May 1978 the
British and Irish governments issued a joint statement in
Dublin which said *inter alia*: 'The British and Irish Governments have a different approach in the search for a long-term
solution for peace and stability in Northern Ireland'. Yet two
years later they embarked on a process which was to culminate
in the Anglo-Irish Agreement and which was to be endorsed
happily by the American administration.

There may, however, be simpler explanations. There can be
little doubt that the Reagan administration has invested much
time and money in countering the network of international
terrorism. One of his most ardent supporters in that and other
policies has been Mrs Thatcher. It may be asserted that Irish
terrorist organizations do not play a notable role on the international scene but, given the attempt on Mrs Thatcher's life at
Brighton and given that it is acknowledged that IRA funding
comes from the United States, it would be surprising if the two
leaders did not co-operate in this sphere. And if the job is to be
done thoroughly then the assistance of the Irish authorities is
called for, something which is recognized in the Anglo-Irish
Agreement.

A second explanation predates President Reagan. It is the
concern for human rights issues enunciated by President
Carter. Irish Americans were not slow in drawing attention to
what they perceived as the lack of certain rights in Northern
Ireland. These included the most fundamental such as the Provisional claim to the right to self-determination whereby the
people of the island of Ireland should settle its constitutional
destiny. At a more mundane but very emotive level they
included charges of judicial prejudice and job discrimination
against the catholic minority. Thus there was the sustained
campaign against an extradition bill involving the UK and USA

which would have enabled the American authorities to return suspected IRA terrorists to the British jurisdiction for trial. The campaign to block the bill received widespread publicity because it was being fought out at the Senate Foreign Relations Committee level. And at the level of state legislatures we have the continuing battle over the McBride principles. All of this gives publicity to the Irish cause and has managed to embarrass both the British and American authorities from time to time. It is inevitable that in a society as highly tuned to the professional lobbyist as the United States these issues play a more dominant part than they would in Britain. In these circumstances there need not be any sinister motives for the relatively keen interest taken by the most powerful state in the world. The kinship network on both sides of the divide and the willingness of both Britain and Ireland to work in harmony produce conditions which permit the US to get involved.

Human rights have also played a part in provoking greater European involvement. On 16 December 1971 the Irish government filed with the European Commission on Human Rights an interstate application in accordance with Article 24 of the European Convention for the Protection of Human Rights and Fundamental Freedoms concerned with the treatment of a number of internees. It was not adopted until 25 January 1976. The Irish were able to claim a victory of sorts but there was little doubt that the matter had created animosity between the two states. In general Ireland used 'Europe' in a less controversial manner although that was not the way it was viewed by loyalists. Document 3696, for example, which was debated before the Council of Europe on 29 January 1976 affirmed that

> just as there is an Irish dimension ... there is a European
> dimension which can be seen at three different levels (a) British
> and Irish membership of the Council ... established, inter alia,
> to guarantee the principle of democracy and human rights ...
> thus [it would be] inconsistent if that organisation did not con-
> sider the problems of Northern Ireland as a common European
> experience (b) the Council of Europe has an interest in matters

concerning legislation, and the administration and judicial practices obtaining in Northern Ireland (c) common membership of the EEC which imposed upon them an even higher degree of obligation to cooperate than is the case between sovereign states in general.

The document came down unequivocally in favour of 'strong coalition government' which should develop 'technical, social and economic' co-operation between North and South. It was unanimously approved by the Political Affairs Committee.

The Council of Europe did not carry too much weight and it is doubtful if the document made any significant impact. The same could not be said, however, for the Haagerup Report, drawn up for the European Parliament by a Danish MEP, Neils Haagerup. Initially his appointment was opposed in Britain on the grounds that any investigation would be an unwarranted interference in the internal affairs of the United Kingdom, but when the report was published British Conservatives abstained in the European Parliament rather than vote against it as many of them had been urged. This might suggest a more enlightened and broader attitude than hitherto, because while the preamble to the report accepted that 'the European Community has no competence to make proposals for changes in the Constitution of Northern Ireland', none the less it did make several interesting suggestions. It called, for example, for the Community to assume greater responsibility for the economic and social development of the province; it encouraged closer Anglo-Irish co-operation and a powersharing form of government in Northern Ireland. The muted British response was surprising and it may be interpreted as an acceptance that solutions to the problem were to be found in a broader context than merely within the province. After all, Haagerup was published in 1984, prior to the New Ireland Forum Report and as the Anglo-Irish process was gathering momentum.

It was possible, however, to construe the Haagerup Report as part of a carefully devised pattern. The tenor of his remarks added fuel to the conspiracy theories. It was noticeable that the most articulate unionist spokesman, Enoch Powell, was also vehemently against the UK joining the European Community. One of the reasons, moreover, why the Republic sought membership was the belief that accession could create a more positive Anglo-Irish outlook through the theme of functional co-operation. The psychological impact on the Republic may have been such that it began to see itself as a co-ordinate and not subordinate unit in the islands. It meant that Anglo-Irish relations were not quite so obsessional a part of Irish foreign policy as they had been at the start of the 1970s. And if one looks at Irish trading figures since entry there has been a significant shift away from almost total dependence on the British market.

But there were political overtones. The European Commission's decision to designate the entire island of Ireland as a single region in the planning of regional policy produced the following reaction from Mr Powell. Speaking in December 1976 he declared that those who supposed that on the continent of Europe there would be either sympathy or understanding or patience for the million British subjects in Ulster who obstinately affirm they are part of the United Kingdom know nothing about Europe and Europeans. 'As the member states are absorbed into the new European State as provinces' he predicted, 'I will tell you what one of those provinces will be. It will be the Province of Ireland, already the official name for the Irish Republic in the documents and language of the EEC.' That was speculation. The reality has been that European integration has been much slower than its architects intended, and only the most starry-eyed optimists now look forward to proper political integration. Indeed, one of the stumbling blocks has been the Republic's insistence that it is a neutral country. This is not the place to examine the validity of that claim, simply to report its capability to impede political integration. Similarly, Ireland's decision to enter the European Monetary System (EMS) in 1979 and Britain's decision to remain outside has had the inevitable consequence of widening the division between North and South. Before EMS entry both parts of Ireland enjoyed the same currency arrangements, but now that the Irish 'punt' has become part of the European basket its rate of exchange fluctuates with that of sterling, thereby strengthening the symbolism of the border.

Another factor, at least in the early days of the Troubles, was the deployment of large numbers of the British army in close proximity to a land border which stretches for over 300 miles. Their presence created tensions which might have provoked an international incident. The Irish complained, for example, of forty-seven border incursions and twenty-seven overflights by the British between August 1969 and early 1972. In a special Dail debate in October 1971 the Taoiseach, Mr Lynch, warned that 'if there are repeated and more serious incursions by the British army across the border it may be necessary to seize the U.N. of this issue as a threat to international peace'.

The international dimension, therefore, could be either benign or malign but probably not neutral. Certainly from early on the Irish recognized, sometimes naïvely, its positive features. Even before European accession the Taoiseach was offering the unionist prime minister Brian Faulkner the availability of Ireland's collective experience and knowledge of European affairs. The offer was accepted in principle and talks at senior-official level were initiated. Garret FitzGerald, as Minister for Foreign Affairs after March 1973, went so far as to promote the regional fund interest of both North and South at a council of ministers meeting in November 1974. He was to be rebutted by both the British government and by unionist politicians. Fianna Fail ministers played the same card when they came back into office after 1977. Michael O'Kennedy went on the offensive in 1979 when he described Northern Ireland as 'the last remaining problem in the Community for peace, it is an exception to the pattern in the rest of the EEC. *The goodwill in Europe and the United States is there to be tapped to support a return to normal politics in the North*'.

Beyond the European and American dimensions the picture has been patchy. Only two international statesmen, both of whom fused temporal positions with spiritual leadership, Pope Paul VI and Archbishop Makarios, dared to speak of Irish unity. Others were more controversial: the Chilean dictator,

President Pinochet, expressed concern at the existence of concentration camps in Ulster, and the Ugandan leader, Idi Amin, once demanded a briefing on Northern Ireland from the British High Commissioner in Kampala.

All of this is simply to say that there was and is an international dimension, but that its positive qualities were largely ignored until the signing of the Anglo-Irish Agreement. It is not too difficult to see why it had not come into play much earlier. From a British perspective, to acknowledge the dimension was to accept that Northern Ireland was not a purely internal affair. Unionists were inclined to see it as gross interference and even as a Popish plot and in any case not to the advantage of the loyalist population. The international community, singly or collectively, was reluctant to intervene in a dispute between two friendly powers, other than to offer whatever humanitarian assistance it could muster. There was, too, the well-recognized principle of sovereignty whereby one did not intervene in another's grief. Besides no state was without its blemishes and would not want these held up before the international community. Ireland was learning to come to terms with the nature of the problem for many years before it could even contemplate organizing others in a systematic manner on its behalf.

Much of that is past history. The position remains that any support for reconciliation from outside the archipelago has to be construed as constructive and not interference. The potential for such constructive co-operation should not be underestimated.

8 Conclusion

There are simple solutions to the problem of Northern Ireland, such as 'Brits out', full integration in the United Kingdom or independence, with or without repartition, but these are only for the simple-minded. 'Brits out' begs the question of who exactly the 'Brits' are: does this group merely comprise members of the administration and security forces who were recruited in Great Britain, or does it include all those who still see themselves as 'British'? This latter group might include over a million people; more than one-fifth of the population of the island. Even the Provisionals recognize that there would have to be a phased dismantling of the links with the rest of the United Kingdom, and most plans which aim at the 'reunification' of Ireland assume a continuance of the British subvention for some years. Unionists regard 'Brits out' as a deeply insulting proposal since they believe that their rights to live in Ireland and to remain within the United Kingdom are as well-founded as those of any nationalist. Indeed, they might argue that it was extreme nationalists who partitioned Ireland in the first place by seceding from the UK. If 'Brits out' refers only to the British army (with or without its Irish soldiers) and implies also the dismantling of the RUC, then it is likely that renewed large-scale sectarian violence would ensue.

Throughout the Troubles the level of loyalist-inspired violence has been restricted by the fact that however unhappy the protestant community may have been with the specifics of British political and security policy, their basic requirement – the maintenance of the Union – is still met by London, and has been guaranteed, so long as a majority of the population approve, by both the British and Irish governments. Many protestants loyally serve in the police and the UDR, but if the British government were unilaterally to abandon Northern Ireland many of these people might be prepared to defend their community and their status by armed force. The restraints on violence which are provided by the presence of the British army, moreover, would be removed and the way could be open to a bloodbath.

This would also be a route towards 'independence'. In the aftermath of the Anglo-Irish Agreement some loyalists have contemplated independence as the only honourable course. It is difficult to see how this option could ever be taken seriously except *in extremis*. Northern Ireland is so small and so economically disadvantaged that living standards would drop catastrophically if it became independent, unless, of course, London was prepared to continue its subvention. It has been suggested that a measure of repartition might ease some of the province's communal problems, but no amount of tinkering about with the border can help the 100,000 or so catholics in Belfast who would inevitably remain inside Northern Ireland.

Full integration with the rest of the United Kingdom has latterly become a widely-canvassed option. The 'Campaign for Equal Citizenship' which backed Robert McCartney's attempt to win a Westminster seat in June 1987 on a 'Real Unionist' ticket argues that the only way to take the border out of politics is to establish Northern Ireland firmly and permanently as an integral part of the United Kingdom and to put aside any notions that the province might ever become part of an independent Ireland. Coupled with this proposal is the call for the main British political parties to organize in Northern Ireland and recruit members in the province. There is some strength in the argument that Northern Ireland is politically disenfranchised since voters in the province may not join the Conservative Party or the Labour Party, and have no opportunity to vote for candidates put up by either side. But the political advantages which *might* accrue to Northern Ireland by a change in this respect are far outweighed by the practical costs which the

British parties would suffer by doing so. The Labour Party is in any case officially committed to the idea of a united Ireland and most British Conservatives have long since ceased to view Ulster Unionists as natural allies, a change of mind to which Ulstermen themselves have powerfully contributed. The unedifying spectacle of loyalist leaders physically attacking the Secretary of State for Northern Ireland – as happened after the Anglo-Irish Agreement – or of MPs such as Ian Paisley accusing Ministers of the Crown of being 'traitors' is only likely to confirm British political parties in the wisdom of keeping Northern Ireland at arm's length.

British policy towards Northern Ireland since 1921 has in effect been designed with precisely that end in mind. The whole point of Lloyd George's Irish settlement – the establishment of the Irish Free State (now the Republic) and Northern Ireland – was to take the Irish question out of British politics, which it had bedevilled for more than fifty years. This policy succeeded until 1968–9 when the violence in the province once more thrust Irish politics on to the British political agenda. The consistent policy of each British administration since direct rule was imposed in 1972 has been to create some form of powersharing devolved administration. A devolved government will help take Irish affairs off the British agenda, and powersharing might ensure that it stays that way in the long term. This policy, however, has so far failed. The 1974 executive which came closest to succeeding collapsed in the face of powerful loyalist opposition and apparent British indifference. The subsequent inability of the province's political leaders to agree on any other arrangement has led London to the view that Dublin might have a tangible role to play in the Northern Irish political process: hence the Anglo-Irish Agreement, which formally provides such a role and also embodies London's continuing faith in a powersharing solution. Although loyalist reaction to the Agreement was undoubtedly much more vigorous than had been expected, London this time has stood firm in the hope that the unionists might come to accept the framework laid down in the Agreement.

In the meantime London must persevere with direct rule,

which successive opinion polls have shown is the least unacceptable political option. Although Northern Ireland continues to be a political nuisance to the United Kingdom, its retention is not so very costly in global terms. The cost of the Northern Ireland subvention to the British Exchequer, although great, is by no means unbearable. With the Ulsterization of the security effort fewer and fewer regular army soldiers are being killed and wounded. In effect there is, in Reginald Maudling's cynical phrase, an 'acceptable level of violence'. But the corrosive impact of the continuing violence within Northern Ireland itself makes it more and more difficult to envisage long term communal harmony. The level of political violence is what sets the province sharply apart from the rest of western Europe. And any answer to the problem which does not directly address the challenge posed by this violence will inevitably fail.

Since the problem is complex, the 'solution' must be so too. The development of new political structures, such as are envisaged in the Anglo-Irish Agreement, can only provide part of the answer. Such structures in any case are more likely to reflect changing communal attitudes than actually alter them. The government – any government – must provide means by which law and order can acceptably be maintained within the province. The process by which the RUC has become more acceptable to the minority community must be continued and every effort must be made to ensure that all the security forces act in as impartial a fashion as possible. The current government is also well aware that Northern Ireland's continuing economic and social disadvantage contribute towards communal tensions. But the problem here is circular. While high levels of unemployment may increase the likelihood of violence, continued unrest will in turn inhibit new investment. Different administrations at different times have placed the main emphasis on particular aspects of the Northern Ireland problem – political, security or socio-economic – but the fact remains that no one strand can be wholly isolated and that to succeed any policy must take into account the interrelationships between each aspect. Over the years it seems that this is one lesson which has been learned by the administration of Northern Ireland.

The 'Troubles' which we have been discussing are deep-seated indeed, and any resolution of the conflict will only take place over a very long period. It is all too easy to lapse into a helpless pessimism when contemplating the problem and surely even Sisyphus had an easy time of it compared to those concerned with the province's future. In late 1987 four main actors remain on the political stage: Northern Ireland's two communities and the two sovereign governments. London and Dublin have agreed on a framework for progress – the Anglo-Irish Agreement – and this has the support of a majority of the catholics. The loyalists, however, are still out in the cold, and, indeed, are in some disarray. But there appears to be a slow unionist realization that old methods and old clichés are no longer relevant. In short, the Anglo-Irish Agreement has at least made that psychological breakthrough. In constitutional terms the Agreement challenges the rigid concepts of state sovereignty and 'national self-determination' – on both sides – which have blocked political progress in the province. This process, if it continues, might give Northern Ireland its best chance since 1974 of moving towards some sort of acceptable internal accommodation.

Appendix I

Deaths Caused by the Violence in Northern Ireland
1969—1987

Year	RUC	Regular army	UDR	Civilians	Total
1969	1	–	–	12	13
1970	2	–	–	23	25
1971	11	43	5	115	174
1972	17	103	26	321	467
1973	13	58	8	171	250
1974	15	28	7	166	216
1975	11	14	6	216	247
1976	23	14	15	245	297
1977	14	15	14	69	112
1978	10	14	7	50	81
1979	14	38	10	51	113
1980	9	8	9	50	76
1981	21	10	13	54	98
1982	12	21	7	57	97
1983	18	5	10	44	77
1984	8	9	10	37	64
1985	23	2	4	24	53
1986	12	4	8	37	61
1987 (to 31 August)	15	3	7	41	66

Appendix II

Agreement Between the Government of the United Kingdom of Great Britain and Northern Ireland and the Government of the Republic of Ireland

The Government of the United Kingdom of Great Britain and Northern Ireland and the Government of the Republic of Ireland:

Wishing further to develop the unique relationship between their peoples and the close co-operation between their countries as friendly neighbours and as partners in the European Community;

Recognising the major interest of both their countries and, above all, of the people of Northern Ireland in diminishing the divisions there and achieving lasting peace and stability;

Recognising the need for continuing efforts to reconcile and to acknowledge the rights of the two major traditions that exist in Ireland, represented on the one hand by those who wish for no change in the present status of Northern Ireland and on the other hand by those who aspire to a sovereign united Ireland achieved by peaceful means and through agreement;

Reaffirming their total rejection of any attempt to promote political objectives by violence or the threat of violence and their determination to work together to ensure that those who adopt or support such methods do not succeed;

Recognising that a condition of genuine reconciliation and dialogue between unionists and nationalists is mutual recognition and acceptance of each other's rights;

Recognising and respecting the identities of the two communities in Northern Ireland, and the right of each to pursue its aspirations by peaceful and constitutional means;

Reaffirming their commitment to a society in Northern Ireland in which all may live in peace, free from discrimination and intolerance, and with the opportunity for both communities to participate fully in the structures and processes of government; Have accordingly agreed as follows:

Status of Northern Ireland

Article 1

The two Governments

(a) affirm that any change in the status of Northern Ireland would only come about with the consent of a majority of the people of Northern Ireland;

(b) recognise that the present wish of a majority of the people of Northern Ireland is for no change in the status of Northern Ireland;

(c) declare that, if in the future a majority of the people of Northern Ireland clearly wish for and formally consent to the establshment of a united Ireland, they will introduce and support in the respective Parliaments legislation to give effect to that wish.

The Intergovernmental Conference

Article 2

(a) There is hereby established, within the framework of the Anglo-Irish Intergovernmental Council set up after the meeting between the two Heads of Government on 6 November 1981, an Intergovernmental Conference (hereinafter referred to as "the Conference"), concerned with Northern Ireland and with relations between the two parts of the island of Ireland, to deal, as set out in this Agreement, on a regular basis with
  (i) political matters;
  (ii) security and related matters;
  (iii) legal matters, including the administration of justice;
  (iv) the promotion of cross-border co-operation.

(b) The United Kingdom Government accept that the Irish Government will put forward views and proposals on matters the Conference in so far as those matters are not the responsibility of a devolved administration in Northern Ireland. In the interest of promoting peace and stability, determined efforts shall be made through the Conference to resolve any differences. The Conference will be mainly concerned with Northern Ireland; but some of the matters under consideration will involve co-operative action in both parts of the island of Ireland, and possibly also in Great Britain. Some of the proposals considered in respect of Northern Ireland may also be found to have application by the Irish Government. There is no derogation from the sovereignty of either the United Kingdom Government or the Irish Government, and each retains responsibility for the decisions and administration of government within its own jurisdiction.

Article 3

The Conference shall meet at Ministerial or official level, as required. The business of the Conference will thus receive attention at the highest level. Regular and frequent Ministerial meetings shall be held; and in particular special meetings shall be convened at the request of either side. Officials may meet in subordinate groups. Membership of the Conference and of sub-groups shall be small and flexible. When the Conference meets at Ministerial level the Secretary of State for Northern Ireland and an Irish Minister designated as the Permanent Irish Ministerial Representative shall be joint Chairmen. Within the framework of the Conference other British and Irish Ministers may hold or attend meetings as appropriate; when legal matters are under consideration the Attorneys General may attend. Ministers may be accompanied by their officials and their professional advisers: for example, when questions of security policy or security co-operation are being discussed, they may be accompanied by the Chief Constable of the Royal Ulster Constabulary and the Commissioner of the Garda Siochana; or when questions of economic or social policy or co-operation are being discussed, they may be accompanied by officials of the relevant Departments. A Secretariat shall be established by the two Governments to service the Conference on a continuing basis in the discharge of its functions as set out in this Agreement.

Article 4

(a) In relation to matters coming within its field of activity, the Conference shall be a framework within which the United Kingdom Government and the Irish Government work together
  (i) for the accommodation of the rights and identities of the two traditions which exist in Northern Ireland; and
  (ii) for peace, stability and prosperity throughout the island of Ireland by promoting reconciliation, respect

for human rights, co-operation against terrorism and the development of economic, social and cultural co-operation.

(b) It is the declared policy of the United Kingdom Government that responsibility in respect of certain matters within the powers of the Secretary of State for Northern Ireland should be devolved within Northern Ireland on a basis which would secure widespread acceptance throughout the community. The Irish Government support that policy.

(c) Both Governments recognise that devolution can be achieved only with the co-operation of constitutional representatives within Northern Ireland of both traditions there. The Conference shall be a framework within which the Irish Government may put forward views and proposals on the modalities of bringing about devolution in Northern Ireland, in so far as they relate to the interests of the minority community.

Political Matters

Article 5

(a) The Conference shall concern itself with measures to recognize and accommodate the rights and identities of the two traditions in Northern Ireland, to protect human rights and to prevent discrimination. Matters to be considered in this area include measures to foster the cultural heritage of both traditions, changes in electoral arrangements, the use of flags and emblems, the avoidance of economic and social discrimination and the advantages and disadvantages of a Bill of Rights in some form in Northern Ireland.

(b) The discussion of these matters shall be mainly concerned with Northern Ireland, but the possible application of any measures pursuant to this Article by the Irish Government in their jurisdiction shall not be excluded.

(c) If it should prove impossible to achieve and sustain devolution on a basis which secures widespread acceptance in Northern Ireland, the Conference shall be a framework within which the Irish Government may, where the interests of the minority community are significantly or especially affected, put forward views on proposals for major legislation and on major policy issues, which are within the purview of the Northern Ireland Departments and which remain the responsibility of the Secretary of State for Northern Ireland.

Article 6

The Conference shall be a framework within which the Irish Government may put forward views and proposals on the role and composition of bodies appointed by the Secretary of State for Northern Ireland or by departments subject to his direction and control including

the Standing Advisory Commission on Human Rights;
the Fair Employment Agency;
the Equal Opportunities Commission;
the Police Authority for Northern Ireland;
the Police Complaints Board.

Security and Related Matters

Article 7

(a) The Conference shall consider
   (i) security policy;
   (ii) relations between the security forces and the community;
   (iii) prisons policy.

(b) The Conference shall consider the security situation at its regular meetings and thus provide an opportunity to address policy issues, serious incidents and forthcoming events.

(c) The two Governments agree that there is a need for a programme of special measures in Northern Ireland to improve relations between the security forces and the community, with the object in particular of making the security forces more readily accepted by the nationalist community. Such a programme shall be developed, for the Conference's consideration, and may include the establishment of local consultative machinery, training in community relations, crime prevention schemes involving the community, improvements in arrangements for handling complaints, and action to increase the proportion of members of the minority in the Royal Ulster Constabulary. Elements of the programme may be considered by the Irish Government suitable for application within their jurisdiction.

(d) The Conference may consider policy issues relating to prisons. Individual cases may be raised as appropriate, so that information can be provided or inquiries instituted.

Legal Matters, Including the Administration of Justice

Article 8

The Conference shall deal with issues of concern to both countries relating to the enforcement of the criminal law. In particular it shall consider whether there are areas of the criminal law applying in the North and in the South respectively which might with benefit be harmonised. The two Governments agree on the importance of public confidence in the administration of justice. The Conference shall seek, with the help of advice from experts as appropriate, measures which would give substantial expression to this aim, considering inter alia the possibility of mixed courts in both jurisdictions for the trial of certain offences. The Conference shall also be concerned with policy aspects of extradition and extra-territorial jurisdiction as between North and South.

Cross-Border Co-operation on Security, Economic, Social and Cultural Matters

Article 9

(a) With a view to enhancing cross-border co-operation on security matters, the Conference shall set in hand a programme of work to be undertaken by the Chief Constable of the Royal Ulster Constabulary and the Commissioner of the Garda Siochana and, where appropriate, groups of officials, in such areas as threat assessments, exchange of information, liaison structures, technical co-operation, training of personnel, and operational resources.

(b) The Conference shall have no operational responsibilities; responsibility for police operations shall remain with the heads of the respective police forces, the Chief Constable of the Royal Ulster Constabulary maintaining his links with the Secretary of State for Northern Ireland and the Commissioner of the Garda Siochana his links with the Minister for Justice.

Article 10

(a) The two Governments shall co-operate to promote the economic and social development of those areas of both parts of Ireland which have suffered most severely from the consequences of the instability of recent years, and shall consider the possibility of securing international support for this work.

(b) If it should prove impossible to achieve and sustain devolution on a basis which secures widespread acceptance in Northern Ireland, the Conference shall be a framework for the promotion of co-operation between the two parts of Ireland concerning cross-border aspects of economic, social and cultural matters in relation to which the

Secretary of State for Northern Ireland continues to exercise authority.

(c) If responsibility is devolved in respect of certain matters in the economic, social or cultural areas currently within the responsibility of the Secretary of State for Northern Ireland, machinery will need to be established by responsible authorities in the North and South for practical co-operation in respect of cross-border aspects of these issues.

Arrangements for Review

Article 11

At the end of three years from signature of this agreement, or earlier if requested by either Government, the working of the Conference shall be reviewed by the two Governments to see whether any changes in the scope and nature of its activities are desirable.

Interparliamentary Relations

Article 12

It will be for Parliamentary decision in Westminster and in Dublin whether to establish an Anglo-Irish Parliamentary body of the kind adumbrated in the Anglo-Irish Studies Report of November 1981. The two Governments agree that they would give support as appropriate to such a body, if it were to be established.

Final Clauses

Article 13

This Agreement shall enter into force on the date on which the two Governments exchange notifications of their acceptance of this Agreement.

[Signed at Hillsborough Castle, Northern Ireland, by Mrs Margaret Thatcher and Dr Garret Fitzgerald, 15 November 1985]

Outline Chronology

1912–14 Home Rule crisis: formation of unionist Ulster Volunteeer Force and nationalist Irish Volunteers; passage of Home Rule Act, but operation postponed by outbreak of First World War.

1916 Easter Rising in Dublin.

1919–21 Anglo-Irish war, during which Ireland was partitioned into Northern Ireland and what became known as the Irish Free State following the Anglo-Irish Treaty of December 1921.

1937 New constitution promulgated in Dublin asserting jurisdiction over the whole island of Ireland.

1949 Irish Republic established. Westminster passed Ireland Act affirming that a change in the constitutional status of the North can only occur with the consent of the Northern Ireland parliament.

1956–62 Sporadic IRA campaign along the Border.

1963 Terence O'Neill became prime minister of Northern Ireland and began modest series of reforms.

1968 Civil rights campaign began in summer, continuing with marches and demonstrations to end of year.

1969 Rioting in Londonderry and Belfast during August; army deployed on peacekeeping duties. Provisionals (PIRA) broke away from official IRA.

1970 Ulster Defence Regiment inaugurated to replace 'B' Specials; SDLP formed.

1971 First soldier killed by PIRA; internment without trial began, followed by widespread rioting.

1972 Thirteen men shot dead by army in Londonderry (Bloody Sunday) on 30 January; UK Embassy in Dublin subsequently burnt down. N. Ireland government resigned after Heath announced transfer of law and order to Westminster. Direct rule established. Nine killed and 130 injured by 19 PIRA bombs in Belfast (Bloody Friday) on 21 July.

1973 Sunningdale conference marked establishment of power-sharing: British, Irish and Northern Irish representatives affirmed that constitutional status of Northern Ireland could only be changed by consent of Protestant majority and agreed to set up a Council of Ireland.

1974 Power-sharing executive of Faulkner (Chief Executive) unionists, SDLP and Alliance formally took office. In May UWC strike caused Executive to collapse.

1975 Phasing out of internment.

1976 Widely supported 'Peace People' demonstrations raised hopes of community reconciliation, but proved to be only a temporary emotional expression of frustration at continuing violence.

1977 'Ulsterisation' policy introduced; abortive Loyalist strike protesting against security policy.

1978 Republican prisoners at Maze prison launched 'dirty protest' in support of better prison conditions.

1979 Conservative Northern Ireland spokesman Airey Neave murdered by INLA bomb at House of Commons. PIRA bombers killed 18 soldiers near Warrenpoint, Co. Down, and assassinated Lord Mountbatten near his holiday home in the Republic.

1980 Mrs Thatcher and Charles Haughey (Irish Prime Minister) reached agreement on 'new and closer political co-operation'. Republican prisoners in H-Blocks of Maze Prison began 'fast unto death' in support of 'political status', but call off protest at New Year.

1981 Bobby Sands began new hunger strike campaign and was followed at regular intervals by further hunger strikers. Sands died on 66th day. 9 further hunger strikers died between May and Aug before campaign was called off.

1982 Provisional Sinn Fein polled 10% of votes in N. Ireland Assembly elections.

1983 Fourteen UVF men jailed after first 'supergrass' trial. Just before Christmas PIRA car bomb at Harrods store in London killed 5 and injured 80.

1984 New Ireland Forum Report recommended unity by consent. President Reagan in Dublin condemned the use of violence in Northern Ireland. Trawler *Marita Ann* captured with large cargo of PIRA arms off west coast of Ireland. Bomb at Grand Hotel Brighton during Conservative Party Conference killed 5 people.

1985 RUC and Protestant demonstrators clashed violently over re-routing of traditional parades away from Catholic areas. PIRA campaign against businessmen who trade with the security forces. Anglo-Irish Agreement signed on 15 Nov. by British and Irish prime ministers at Hillsborough Castle, county Down; massive loyalist demonstrations against Agreement follow.

1986 Unionists lost one seat to SDLP in 15 by-elections caused by their mass resignation from the House of Commons in protest against the Agreement. SDLP took votes from Provisional candidates. Loyalist campaign against Agreement marked by non-co-operation in local government, marches, heightened paramilitary activity and attacks on off-duty RUC personnel and their families. Northern Ireland Assembly wound up.

1987 Charles Haughey, leader of Fianna Fail, forms government in Dublin after general election in which Sinn Fein won less than 2% of vote. 12 people died in internal INLA feud which began at the end of 1986; 8 PIRA men were killed during attack on police station at Loughgall, county Armagh. Sinn Fein won 9% of Northern Ireland vote in United Kingdom general election.

Dramatis Personae

ADAMS, GERRY (b. 1949). Republican activist and Sinn Fein Westminster MP for West Belfast since 1983.

BARRY, PETER (b. 1928). Fine Gael politician and Foreign Minister of the Irish Republic 1982–7.

BRADFORD, REVEREND ROBERT (1941–81). Ulster Unionist MP for South Belfast assassinated by Provisional IRA in November 1981.

CARSON, SIR EDWARD (1854–1935). Unionist MP 1892–1921 and leader of opposition to Irish home rule.

CHICHESTER-CLARK, JAMES (b. 1923). Leader of Ulster Unionist Party and Prime Minister of Northern Ireland 1969–71.

CRAIG, SIR JAMES (LORD CRAIGAVON) (1871–1940). Unionist leader and first prime minister of Northern Ireland 1921–40.

CRAIG, WILLIAM (b. 1924). Unionist MP at Stormont 1960–72 (cabinet minister 1962–8). Westminster MP 1974–9. Only leader of Vanguard Unionist Progressive Party 1973–8.

DE VALERA, EAMON (1882–1975). Veteran Irish republican leader. President of Irish Republic 1959–73.

FAULKNER, BRIAN (1921–77). Leader of Ulster Unionist Party and Prime Minister of Northern Ireland 1971–2. Chief Executive in powersharing administration in 1974. Leader of Unionist Party of Northern Ireland 1974–6.

FITT, GERARD (b. 1926). Westminster MP for West Belfast 1966–83. Leader of Social Democratic and Labour Party from its foundation in 1970 to 1979. Member of powersharing executive in 1974. Created Lord Fitt in 1983.

FITZGERALD, GARRET (b. 1926). Taoiseach (prime minister) of the

Irish Republic 1981–March 1982 and December 1982–7. Leader of Fine Gael Party 1977–87.

HAUGHEY, CHARLES (b. 1925). Taoiseach (prime minister) of the Irish Republic 1979–81, 1982 and since 1987. Leader of Fianna Fail party since 1979.

HERMON, SIR JOHN (b. 1929). Chief Constable of the Royal Ulster Constabulary since 1980.

HUME, JOHN (b. 1937). Westminster MP for Foyle since 1983. Leader of Social Democratic and Labour Party since 1979. Member of powersharing executive in 1974.

LYNCH, JACK (b. 1917). Fianna Fail politician and Taoiseach (prime minister) of the Irish Republic 1966–73 and 1977–9.

MACBRIDE, SEAN (b. 1904). IRA leader in 1920s and 1930s. Cabinet minister in Dublin 1948–51. Winner of Nobel and Lenin Peace Prizes.

MACGUINNESS, MARTIN (b. 1950). Republican activist and Sinn Fein Northern Ireland Assembly member for Londonderry, 1982–6.

MACSTIOFAIN, SEAN (b. 1928). Chief of Staff of Provisional IRA 1970–2.

MCCUSKER, HAROLD (b. 1940). Deputy leader of Ulster Unionist Party since 1982 and Westminster MP for Armagh/Upper Bann since 1974.

MOLYNEAUX, JAMES (b. 1920). Westminster MP since 1970. Leader of Ulster Unionist Party since 1979.

MORRISON, DANNY (b. 1953). Sinn Fein director of publicity and Northern Ireland Assembly member for Mid-Ulster 1982–6.

O'NEILL, TERENCE (b. 1914). Leader of Ulster Unionist Party and Prime Minister of Northern Ireland, 1963–9.

OLDFIELD, SIR MAURICE (1915–80). Head of Secret Intelligence Service (MI6) 1965–77. Northern Ireland Security Co-ordinator 1979–80.

PAISLEY, IAN (b. 1926). Moderator of Free Presbyterian Church. Founder and leader of Democratic Unionist Party since 1971. Westminster MP for North Antrim from 1970.

POWELL, ENOCH (b. 1912). Conservative MP 1950–74 and minister of health 1960–3. Unionist MP for South Down at Westminster 1974–87.

RICHARDS, SIR BROOKS (b. 1918). Northern Ireland Security Co-ordinator 1980–2.

ROBINSON, PETER (b. 1948). Deputy leader of the Democratic Unionist Party 1979–87 and Westminster MP for East Belfast since 1979.

TYRIE, ANDY (b. 1940). Commander of the Ulster Defence Association since 1973.

WEST, HARRY (b. 1917). Stormont MP 1954–72 (cabinet minister 1960–6 and 1971–2). Westminster MP February–October 1974. Leader of Ulster Unionist Party 1974–9.

Further Reading

Arthur, Paul, *The Government and Politics of Northern Ireland* (Longman, 2nd edn updated, 1987).

Bew, Paul and Patterson, Henry, *The British State and the Ulster Crisis: from Wilson to Thatcher* (Verso, 1986).

Boyle, Kevin and Hadden, Tom, *Ireland: A Positive Proposal* (Penguin, 1985).

Buchanan, R. H. and Walker, B. M. (eds), *Province, City and People: Belfast and Its Region* (Greystone Books/Northern Ireland Committee of the British Association for the Advancement of Science, 1987).

Buckland, Patrick, *The Northern Ireland Question 1886–1986* (Historical Association, 1987).

Fanning, Ronan, *Independent Ireland* (Helicon, 1983).

Flackes, W. D., *Northern Ireland: A Political Directory 1968–83* (Ariel, 1983).

Harkness, David, *Northern Ireland since 1920* (Helicon, 1983).

Jeffery, Keith (ed.), *The Divided Province: The Troubles in Northern Ireland 1969–85* (Orbis, 1985).

Kee, Robert, *The Green Flag* (Weidenfeld and Nicolson, 1972).

Miller, David, *Queen's Rebels* (Gill and Macmillan, 1978).

Murphy, Dervla, *A Place Apart* (Penguin, 1979).

Rea, D. (ed.), *Models of Political Co-operation* (Gill and Macmillan, 1982).

Stewart, A. T. Q., *The Narrow Ground* (Faber and Faber, 1977).

Index

(Northern Ireland is abbreviated as NI)

Adams, Gerry, 38, 39, 43, 45, 113
Alliance Party, 8, 12, 16, 52, 61
Amin, Idi, 92
Anglo-Irish Agreement, 13, 32, 111;
    background to, 77–8;
    significance, 2; terms of, 16–19,
    75–6, 99–108
army, regular: attacks on, 63;
    deployment in NI, 9–10, 64, 76,
    91; *see also* security policy, Special
    Air Service Regiment, Ulster
    Defence Regiment
Atkins, Humphry, 14, 86
Australia, 17

Barry, Peter, 58, 113
Belfast, 9, 18, 19, 23
Bennett, Joseph, 73
Biaggi, Congressman Mario, 84
'Bloody Friday', 66, 110
'Bloody Sunday', 14, 110
Bradford, Rev. Robert, 58, 113
Brighton, bomb at Grand Hotel, 1,
    67, 87
'B-Specials' (Ulster Special
    Constabulary), 6, 11
Brookeborough, Lord, 46

Campaign for Democracy in Ulster
    (CDU), 7
Campaign for Equal Citizenship,
    18, 94–5

Canada, 17
Caradon, Lord, 81
Carey, Hugh, 85
Carrington, Lord, 87
Carson, Sir Edward, 36, 47, 55, 78,
    113
Carter, Jimmy, 83
catholic(s), 3, 22, 25; employment,
    29; politics, 33–45; population in
    NI, 23; social disadvantage, 30–1
Channon, Paul, 38
Chichester-Clark, Major James, 9,
    54, 113
Council of Europe, 88–9
Council of Ireland, 12
Craig, Sir James, 36, 47, 79, 113
Craig, William, 13, 46, 47–8, 53, 113
Creasey, Lt-Gen Sir Timothy, 71

De Lorean Motor Company, 28, 29
Democratic Unionist Party (DUP):
    origins and electoral fortunes,
    51–60; reaction to Anglo-Irish
    Agreement, 18–19, 50; in UUUC,
    49; *see also* Protestant Unionist
    Party
Derry/Londonderry, 3;
    demonstrations and riots, 5–6, 9,
    15; gerrymandering, 5
de Valera, Eamon, 79, 80, 113
Diplock Courts, 69, 75
'Downing Street Declaration', 11

economy, 26–8
education, 24–5
European Commission on Human Rights, 88
European Economic Community (EEC), 17, 41, 89–91
Ewart-Biggs, Christopher, 15, 68

Fair Employment Act (1976) 30, 31
Faulkner, Brian, 11, 12, 54, 79, 91, 113
Ferguson, Richard, 8
Fianna Fail party, 43, 91
Fine Gael party, 43
Fitt, Gerry, 7, 113
FitzGerald, Garret, 16, 91, 113
Freeland, Lt-Gen Sir Ian, 11
Friends of Ireland Group, 84–5

Garda Siochana, 15
Gibson, Ken, 48
Gibson, Lord Justice, 68
Goulding, Cathal, 63

Haagerup, Neils: report on NI for European Parliament, 42, 89–90
Haughey, Charles, 15, 16, 112, 114
'H-Block' campaign, 15
Heath, Edward, 12, 56
Hermon, Sir John, 71, 114
Hillery, Patrick, 78, 81
Hillsborough Agreement, *see* Anglo-Irish Agreement
housing, 5
Hume, John, 8, 29, 42, 43, 85, 114
hunger strikes (1980–1), 15, 35, 37, 65

Industrial Development Board (IDB), 27
International Fund for Ireland, 17
internment, 12, 73
Ireland, *see* Republic of Ireland
Irish Independence Party, 40
Irish National Caucus, 29, 84
Irish National Liberation Army (INLA), 63–4, 73; *see also* Irish Republican Socialist Party

Irish Republican Army (IRA), 10, 22, 34–5, 37; *see also* Official IRA, Provisional IRA
Irish Republican Socialist Party, 63; *see also* Irish National Liberation Army

Kennedy, Senator Edward, 85

Lawson, Lt-Gen Sir Richard, 71
La Mon House restaurant, 67
Local Enterprise Development Unit, 27
Londonderry, *see* Derry/Londonderry
Lynch, Jack, 78, 114

MacBride, Sean, 29, 114
MacBride Principles, 29–30, 31, 88
McCartney, Robert, 18, 94
McCusker, Harold, 50, 114
McGlinchey, Dominic, 63
McGuinness, Martin, 38, 114
McManus, Father Sean, 84
MacStiofain, Sean, 38, 65–6, 114
Makarios, Archbishop, 91
Maryfield, 17, 19
Mason, Roy, 14
Maudling, Reginald, 46, 96
MI5, 74
Millar, Frank, 50
Molyneaux, James, 18, 58–9, 86–7, 114
Morrison, Danny, 39, 114
Mountbatten, Lord, 15, 68, 71, 110
Moxon-Browne, Edward, 60
Moynihan, Senator Patrick, 85
Murphy, Dervla, 21

National H-Block Committee, 65
Nationalist Party, 8, 40
Neave, Airey, 56, 110
New Ireland Forum, 39, 42–3, 45
New Ulster Political Research Group (NUPRG), 49–50
New Zealand, 17
Noraid (Irish Northern Aid Committee), 84

Northern Ireland: population, 23–4; religious affiliations, 23; solutions to problem, 92–7
Northern Ireland Assembly, 16, 18, 42, 48
Northern Ireland Civil Rights Association (NICRA), 5, 6
Northern Ireland Constitutional Convention, 14, 49, 53, 57
Northern Ireland Labour Party (NILP), 61
Northern Ireland Parliament (Stormont), 7, 8, 11–12, 33

Official IRA, 37, 63, 73; *see also* Irish Republican Army, Workers' Party
O'Kennedy, Michael, 91
Oldfield, Sir Maurice, 71, 114
O'Neill, Captain Terence, 6–8, 25, 35, 47
O'Neill, 'Tip', 85, 86, 109, 114
Orange Order, 6
Orange Volunteers, 13

Paisley, Rev. Ian, 6, 13, 18, 48, 114; fundamentalist politics, 50–1; leadership of DUP, 51, 52–4, 58–9; opposition to Anglo-Irish process, 78–9; and UDA, 57
partition, 32
Peck, Sir John, 81, 82
People's Democracy (PD), 6
Pinochet, President, 92
police, *see* Royal Ulster Constabulary
Pope Paul VI, 91
Portadown, 19
Powell, Enoch, 18, 56, 57, 114; conspiracy theories about NI, 80, 86, 89–90; and EEC, 90
powersharing: executive, 12–13, 14; consistent British policy, 95
Prior, James, 42, 56
Progressive Unionist Party, 50
protestant(s), 3, 6, 22, 93–4; employment, 28–31; politics, 46–61; population in NI, 23; reaction to Anglo-Irish Agreement, 32, 47, 49–50, 70
Protestant Unionist Party, 51; *see also* Democratic Unionist Party
Provisional IRA, 33, 45, 109; and internment, 73; and republican tradition, 36; security threat, 62; strategy and tactics, 64–9; support in USA, 84; talks with British government, 37–8; *see also* Irish Republican Army, Sinn Fein
Provisional Sinn Fein, *see* Sinn Fein

Reagan, Ronald, 17, 85, 87
Rees, Merlyn, 13
religion, 22–3
Republican Sinn Fein, 39
Republic of Ireland: 1916 Proclamation, 35, 36, 37; 1937 Constitution, 34; relations with UK, 77–83; role in NI affairs, 12–13, 14; terrorism in, 14, 15
Richards, Sir Brooks, 71, 115
Robinson, Peter, 50, 115
Royal Ulster Constabulary (RUC), 5, 9, 19, 94; attacks on, 63, 65–8, 70; reform, 11–12; role in security policy, 10–11, 70–71, 74, 96; size, 70; Stalker report, 74; *see also* 'B-Specials', security policy

Sands, Bobby, 111
security policy: and car bombs, 66–7; covert operations, 72, 74; criminalization, 69; cross-border co-operation, 15; direction of, 10–11; house searches, 37; informers and supergrasses, 72–3, 74–5; 'shoot to kill', 74; transferred to London, 12; Ulsterization, 68–71
security statistics, 98
Sinn Fein, 36, 38–40, 42–5, 44, 65
Social Democratic and Labour Party (SDLP), 14, 29, 30, 53, 60, 110; boycotts Assembly, 16; election results, 44; formed, 8;

SDLP (*cont.*)
  policies and development, 40–45;
  policy towards USA, 83; and
  powersharing executive, 12
social policy, 25–6
Special Air-Service (SAS) Regiment,
  72, 74
Stalker, John, 74
Stormont, *see* Northern Ireland
  Parliament
Sunningdale Agreement, 56

Thatcher, Mrs Margaret, 15, 16, 56,
  57, 86, 87
'Third Force', 39, 47
Tighe, Michael, 74
Tyrie, Andy, 49, 115

Ulster Clubs movement, 39, 47
Ulster Covenant (1912), 36
Ulster Defence Association (UDA),
  13, 48–9, 57; *see also* New Ulster
  Political Research Group
Ulster Defence Regiment (UDR),
  11, 110; casualties, 68; character
  of, 70; size, 69–70
Ulster Loyalist Co-ordinating
  Committee, 48
Ulster Special Constabulary
  Association, 13
Ulster Unionist Party (UUP), 5, 7,
  8, 12, 16; reaction to Anglo-Irish
  Agreement, 18–19, 50;
  domination of Stormont, 33–5,

50; in UUUC, 49; electoral
  fortunes and competition with
  DUP, 52–60
Ulster Volunteer Force (UVF), 13,
  36, 47, 48
Ulster Workers' Council (UWC)
  Strike, 13, 14, 39, 47, 53
unemployment, 27
Unionist Party, *see* Ulster Unionist
  Party
United Kingdom, subvention to NI,
  26, 96; relations with Republic of
  Ireland, 77–83
United Nations, 17, 77, 78, 82
United States of America (USA), 17;
  investment in NI, 29–30, 83; Irish
  lobby in, 83–6; and NI human
  rights issues, 87–8; strategic
  interest in Ireland, 80–6
United Ulster Unionist Council
  (UUUC), 12–13, 49, 57

Vance, Cyrus, 87
Vanguard Unionist Party (VUP),
  47–8, 49, 52, 53

West, Harry, 53, 54, 115
Whitelaw, William, 12, 38
Wilson, Harold, 7, 72
Workers' Party, 63; *see also* Official
  IRA

Young, Sir Arthur, 11, 12